CAMBRIDGE
Global English
Workbook

Chris Barker and Libby Mitchell

CAMBRIDGE
UNIVERSITY PRESS

University Printing House, Cambridge CB2 8BS, United Kingdom

Cambridge University Press is part of the University of Cambridge.

It furthers the University's mission by disseminating knowledge in the pursuit of education, learning and research at the highest international levels of excellence.

Information on this title: education.cambridge.org

© Cambridge University Press 2014

This publication is in copyright. Subject to statutory exception and to the provisions of relevant collective licensing agreements, no reproduction of any part may take place without the written permission of Cambridge University Press.

First published 2014
Reprinted 2015

Printed by Multivista Global Ltd, India

ISBN: 978-1107-65771-7

Cambridge University Press has no responsibility for the persistence or accuracy of URLs for external or third-party internet websites referred to in this publication, and does not guarantee that any content on such websites is, or will remain, accurate or appropriate. Information regarding prices, travel timetables, and other factual information given in this work is correct at the time of first printing but Cambridge University Press does not guarantee the accuracy of such information thereafter.

Contents

UNIT 1 Languages of the world
1 My language, your language 4
2 Teach yourself Tok Pisin! 6
3 It's good to learn languages 8

UNIT 2 E-communication
1 Are you a good communicator? 10
2 The future of schools 12
3 I wish I hadn't done that! 14

UNIT 3 Rivers and coasts
1 The Nile 16
2 The water cycle 18
3 Saved by the bell! 20

UNIT 4 Great expeditions
1 *Titanic* 22
2 The Treasure Fleet 24
3 Should we continue to explore space? 26

UNIT 5 Sports and hobbies
1 Sport for all 28
2 At the top of their game 30
3 What are your hobbies? 32

UNIT 6 Entertainment and media
1 What are you into? 34
2 At the circus 36
3 A film review 38

UNIT 7 Household routines
1 In the kitchen 40
2 In my room 42
3 Jobs at home 44

UNIT 8 Habitat interactions
1 Rainforests 46
2 Live and let live 48
3 The food chain 50

UNIT 9 Buildings and structures
1 Brilliant buildings 52
2 Art meets engineering 54
3 School design challenge 56

UNIT 10 Design and shape
1 A bar of chocolate 58
2 What shape is it? 60
3 Classic designs 62

UNIT 11 Personality types
1 What are you really like? 64
2 A teenage millionaire 66
3 The world of soap opera 68

UNIT 12 People and their jobs
1 The world of work 70
2 A day in the life 72
3 What about becoming a …? 74

UNIT 13 Shops and services
1 In the aisles 76
2 The psychology of shopping 78
3 The best present 80

UNIT 14 Possessions and personal space
1 Treasured possessions 82
2 My space 84
3 For sale 86

UNIT 15 Natural disasters
1 Dangerous nature 88
2 Drought in East Africa 90
3 Raising money for charity 92

UNIT 16 Survivors
1 Amazing survival 94
2 Surviving together 96
3 Survival kit 98

UNIT 17 Summer season
1 Summer holidays 100
2 Summer camp in Japan 102
3 A room with a view 104

UNIT 18 Using English
1 King Midas 106
2 The story of Midas 108
3 The performance 110
Grammar reference 112

1 Languages of the world

My language, your language

1 Write the languages for the countries. Look them up on the Internet if you need to.

Country	Main languages
1 New Zealand	English, Maori (New Zealand sign language)
2 Japan	
3 Spain	
4 Germany	
5 France	
6 Italy	
7 Portugal	
8 Brazil	
9 Argentina	
10 Russia	

2 How good are you at languages? Try this quick quiz. (Clue: the answers to questions 2 to 5 are all in Exercise 1, but you can use the Internet to help you.)

1 The words in the speech bubbles all mean the same thing. What is it? _____

2 In Italian, this word can also mean 'Bye'. Which number is it on the globe?

_____

3 This language uses the Cyrillic alphabet. It's number 5 on the globe. What language is it? _____

4 The more formal way of saying number 3 is 'Bonjour'. What language is it?

_____

5 Look at numbers 1 and 2. Which is Spanish and which is Portuguese?

_____

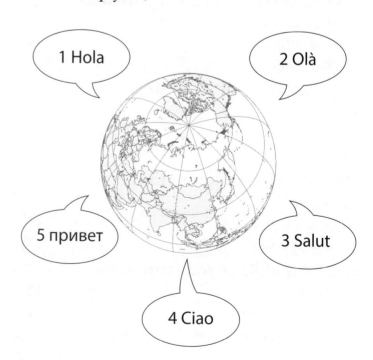

4 Cambridge Global English Stage 8 Workbook

1: Languages of the world

3 Complete the texts with the correct countries and languages.

I'm from Montreal. It's in Quebec which is a province in the east of ¹_____. It belonged to France at one point in its history. So ²_____ is my first language, but I also speak ³_____.

I live in Rabat, the capital of ⁴_____, in North Africa. ⁵_____ and Berber are our official languages. My parents also speak French because they work for a company which has offices in ⁶_____. I speak a little bit of ⁷_____ because my cousins live in Spain and I've been to visit them several times. I learn ⁸_____ at school, but I've never been to a country where it's spoken as a native language.

4 Circle the mistakes. Then write out the sentences correctly.

1 Both my parents speaks English.
_____

2 All my friends likes watching films in English.
_____

3 I've got two cousins who live in Canada, but neither them speaks French.
_____
_____

4 Every my friends want to study at university.
_____

5 I gave each my four cousins a present.
_____

6 I've got two sisters and all of them are good at languages.
_____

5 Rewrite these sentences to make them true for you.

1 Everyone in my family speaks German.
_____

2 I can say 'hello' in three languages.
_____

3 I can count to ten in Spanish and French.
_____

4 Most of us learn English at school. Our grandparents learned French as a foreign language when they were at school.
_____

5 I'd really like to be able to speak Italian because it sounds so nice.
_____

Cambridge Global English Stage 8 Workbook

Teach yourself Tok Pisin!

1 These are the numbers 1 to 10 in Tok Pisin. Write the English translation next to each number.

et _eight_   faiv _____   foa _____   nain _____   seven _____

sikis _____   ten _____   tri _____   tu _____   wan _____

2 Complete the crossword.

Across

2 A pidgin language that has become the mother tongue of a community. (6)
6 The language spoken in Poland. (6)
9 An English-speaking country close to 11 Down. (9)
10 The language of ancient Rome. (5)
12 Russian uses the Cyrillic _____. (8)
14 A language spoken in Southern China and Hong Kong. (9)

Down

1 Speaking two languages. (9)
3 English and French are the _____ languages of Canada. (8)
4 The most important city in a country. (7)
5 All the words that someone knows, learns or uses. (10)
7 The number of people living in a country. (10)
8 Your first language is your _____ language. (6)
11 Papua _____ Guinea. (3)
13 A main language spoken in India. (5)

6 Cambridge Global English Stage 8 Workbook

1: Languages of the world

3 **Rewrite the sentences using *although*.**

1. I speak English quite well, but I find English spelling hard.
   Although I speak English quite well, I find English spelling hard.

2. The islands of Trinidad and Tobago are very close to Venezuela, but English is spoken there, not Spanish.
   _____

3. Welsh settlers first went to Patagonia in 1865, but Welsh is still quite widely spoken in this part of Argentina today.
   _____

4. Chinese is an important world language, but not many schools in Britain teach it.
   _____

5. Shakespeare probably never left England, but several of his plays are set in other countries.
   _____

4 **Match the contrasting ideas and then join them in a sentence with *whereas/while*.**

1. In Britain, the winter months are December, January and February.
2. I'm good at languages.
3. In Argentina, Spanish is spoken.
4. Very few British people speak Dutch.
5. In Japan, the school year starts in April.

In Australia, students start school in January.
In South Africa, winter is from May to July.
Most Dutch people speak English.
My brother's best subjects are Science and Maths.
Portuguese is the language of Brazil.

1. *In Britain, the winter months are December, January and February, whereas in South Africa winter is from May to July.*

_____
_____
_____
_____
_____
_____
_____

It's good to learn languages

1 Complete the interview answers with suitable words.

Is it useful to know another language?

Yes, it is, definitely. Speaking to [1] _someone_ in their own language, even if [2] _____ is only for a short time, [3] _____ that person feel more at ease.
It's [4] _____ useful when you visit another country. [5] _____ to say 'hello' and 'thank you' [6] _____ the language of that country is [7] _____.

So knowing just a few words makes a difference?

Yes, it makes all the difference. [8] _____ may only know a few words [9] _____ people like it when you try [10] _____ speak their language.
If you enjoy [11] _____ or films from another country, it's [12] _____ to be able to understand at [13] _____ a little bit.

Do you speak any other languages?

Well, I'm learning [14] _____ at school. I like being able [15] _____ understand some of the words when [16] _____ hear a Spanish song.

What do you think are the advantages of learning a language?

Studies show [17] _____ learning another language is good for [18] _____.
It improves your brain power and [19] _____ is some evidence to show that [20] _____ who are bilingual live longer.
Knowing [21] _____ language helps you to use your [22] _____ language well. I teach History and [23] _____ find that students who know another [24] _____ have better reading skills and wider [25] _____. And of course, having another language [26] _____ be very helpful for going to [27] _____ or university.

Are you more likely to be successful if you speak the language of the people you do business with?

Yes, you are. For [28] _____, if you work for a Japanese [29] _____ in Europe or America, you really [30] _____ to speak some Japanese. And they [31] _____ that people who use languages in [32] _____ jobs earn about 8% more than [33] _____ who don't use them.

1: Languages of the world

2 Read the tips for learning a language. Which statements in the second column illustrate the advice in the first column? Match them.

1 Don't be afraid of making mistakes.
2 Take the opportunity to listen to the language as much as possible.
3 Watch films and TV in English.
4 Find a way to learn new words and remember them.
5 Practise speaking as much as you can.
6 Test yourself.

a Don't be afraid of reading out loud in your room at home and practising conversations with a friend.
b For example, try to find an English-speaking radio station. You may even find a pop music station – songs are a good way of helping you learn a language.
c It's all part of the learning process. Don't expect to get everything right all the time.
d Read through what you've learned in class. Cover the page and see how much you can remember.
e Try writing them on pieces of paper and stick them around the house.
f You won't understand everything, but it's good to be able to see people speaking as well as hearing them.

3 In your notebook, write answers to the questions, giving your own opinions. Use the phrases from the box in your answers where possible.

| • definitely | • even if | • it's really useful | • it makes all the difference | • a little bit |
| • of course | • more likely to be | • for example | • at ease | |

1 What are the advantages of knowing other languages?
2 Would you like to study in another country in the future?
3 Do you ever feel nervous when you're speaking another language?
4 What's the best way to learn a new language?
5 Are languages as important as the other subjects you learn at school? Why? Why not?
6 If you were teaching an English speaker your language, how would you start?

2 E-communication

Are you a good communicator?

1 Solve the crossword.

Across

4 A phone that you carry with you. (6)
6 To talk informally. (4)
7 When I _____ a message on my mobile, it makes a noise like a bird. (7)
8 It's short for 'application' and you can use it on your mobile. (3)
9 I wanted to make a call on my mobile, but there was no _____. (6)
12 To transfer music, etc. from the Internet to your own computer or mobile device. (8)

Down

1 You need this to connect to the Internet without using wires. (2, 2)
2 An informal diary on 11 *Down*. (4)
3 This describes the computer that you have at home and that you don't carry with you. (7)
5 You need a password to _____ the Internet. (6)
10 A computer that you carry with you. (6)
11 The worldwide web, it's also called 'the net'. (8)

2: E-communication

2 Complete the sentences with the correct prepositions.

• for (x2)   • from   • in   • on   • up   • with (x2)

1 When we're doing a project, we look ___up___ a lot of things _____ the Internet.
2 I don't think it's fair to musicians to download music _____ the Internet _____ free.
3 Can you recommend an app _____ learning to read music?
4 I always take my mobile phone _____ me when I go out.
5 It's easy to keep _____ touch _____ friends using Skype and email.

3 Combine the pairs of sentences using *to*.

1 I wanted to find out the football score. That's why I turned my computer on.
   I turned my computer on to find out the football score.
2 My mum wanted to buy a new mobile phone. That's why she went into town.
   _____
3 I wanted to ask you about the maths homework. That's why I phoned you.
   _____
4 He wanted to find the cinema. That's why he looked at the map on his phone.
   _____
5 I'd like to improve my English. That's why I'm going to spend three weeks in Sydney.
   _____

4 Combine the pairs of sentences using *to/in order (not) to* where possible. Otherwise use *so that* with *could/couldn't* or *would/wouldn't*.

1 My mum bought a new laptop. She wanted to make life easier when she was travelling.
   My mum bought a new laptop to make life easier when she was travelling.
2 Our teacher gave us practice papers. She wanted us to be ready for the exam.
   Our teacher gave us practice papers, so that we would be ready for the exam.
3 I gave my cousin my email address. I wanted her to send me her holiday photos.
   _____
4 I saved up some money. I wanted to buy an iPod.
   _____
5 I put my phone on silent. I didn't want it to disturb anyone.
   _____
6 I took my phone with me. I didn't want to miss your call.
   _____

Cambridge Global English Stage 8 Workbook

The future of schools

1 Label the pictures by reordering the letters.

1 a t s e l i l t e _____

2 s h a p o n d e e h _____

3 r o c i m o n e p h _____

4 c a b m e w _____

5 c a r t e t i n i v e   d r o w a b e i t h

_____   _____

2 Look at the pictures in Exercise 1 and answer the questions.

1 Where do you find number 1 and what does it do?

_____

_____

2 When and why would you wear number 2?

_____

_____

3 What does number 3 do?

_____

_____

4 What does number 4 do?

_____

_____

5 Is number 5 better than an ordinary board? Why?

_____

_____

3 Read the itinerary for the first day of the school ski trip. Then write an account of what will happen. Use the passive.

School ski trip – day 1

6.30 am	coach takes students and teachers from school to the airport
10.00 am	local guide meets us
10.30 am	bus takes us to hotel
12.00	hotel serves lunch
1.00 pm	local ski shop provides skis and boots
1.30 pm	teachers collect lift passes and hand them out to students
2.15 pm	• ski instructors meet students at the Alpine ski lift
	• ski instructors divide students into groups according to ability
2.30 pm	the instructors accompany students to the slopes for their first lesson
4.30 pm	teachers meet students at the bottom of the lift and take them back to the hotel

6.30 am — *Students and teachers will be taken from school to the airport by coach.*

10.00 am — *We will be met …* _____

10.30 am — _____

12.00 — _____

1.00 pm — _____

1.30 pm — _____

2.15 pm — • _____
• _____

2.30 pm — _____

4.30 pm — _____

I wish I hadn't done that!

1 Write captions for the pictures.

Use should have / shouldn't have

1

I should have got here earlier.

2

_____

3

_____

4

_____

Use I wish

5

I wish I hadn't stayed up so late.

6

_____

Use If only

7

If only I'd done some revision.

8

_____

2: E-communication

2 Use the words in the box to complete the text about the advantages and disadvantages of email.

| • arrives | • attachment | • expensive | • junk | • message | • quick |
| • send | • texting | • too | • uses | • virus | • wish |

Advantages of email

It's very ¹_____. You can send a message and it usually ²_____ a few seconds later.
You can ³_____ an email message anywhere in the world.
It's not ⁴_____. It's cheaper than ⁵_____ if you want to send a message to a friend in another country.
And you can send the same ⁶_____ to lots of different people at the same time.

Disadvantages of email

Not everyone ⁷_____ email.
You get quite a lot of ⁸_____ mail from people wanting to sell things. It's really annoying.
Sometimes it's just ⁹_____ quick and easy. You write an email and send it without thinking and then you ¹⁰_____ you hadn't.
An email might have an ¹¹_____ with a ¹²_____, which can really mess up your computer.

3 Read the email. What is wrong with it?

1 Write your comments next to the email. Use *should have* and *shouldn't have*.
2 Correct the spelling, grammar and punctuation.

From: Mandy
To: Gina
Cc:
Subject:

Gina

I got your email I haven't replied because ive been busy.

Anyway DON'T send me emails late at nite, my computer makes a noise when they come in and it's anoying because it wakes me up your just as bad as Nicole. She sends me texts at 2 o'clock in the morning. There realy long and boring.

I wish she wouldnt send them.

Mandy

3 Rivers and coasts

The Nile

1 Read the clues and complete the word puzzle to find the name of the river.

Clues

1. The regular rise and fall in the level of the sea.
2. The kind of water you find in most lakes and rivers.
3. A low flat area of land where a river divides into smaller rivers and into the sea.
4. The place where a river starts.
5. A layer of mud, sand, stones, etc. at the bottom of a river.
6. The flat land between two hills or mountains.
7. Areas of soft, wet land.
8. The wide part of a river where it goes into the sea.
9. Land along the side of a river.
10. A large reptile with sharp teeth.
11. The amount of rain that falls on an area in a particular period of time.
12. The Mediterranean, for example.

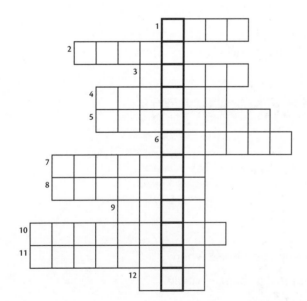

16 Cambridge Global English Stage 8 Workbook

2 Find the words in the text to label the pictures.

> Apart from cereals, fruit and vegetables, plants such as flax and papyrus were grown on the river banks. Flax was made into rope and linen. Papyrus was made into boats, in which you could sail on the river, mats for the house and material on which you could write.

1 flax   2 _____   3 _____

4 _____   5 _____   6 _____

3 Test your knowledge of verb tenses. Circle the correct options in the following text.

People ¹(*are living* / *have lived*) along the banks of the Nile for thousands of years. The ancient Egyptians ²(*planned* / *have planned*) their lives around the life of the river.

Every year in June the river flooded, but when the floods ³(*have gone* / *had gone*), the sediment that ⁴(*is left* / *was left*) behind provided wonderfully fertile soil to grow crops for food. Cereals, vegetables and fruit ⁵(*are growing* / *were grown*) on the banks of the Nile. People could also catch fish in the river. At that time, fish ⁶(*has been* / *was*) the main source of animal protein for most people.

The water cycle

1 Use these words to label the diagram.

| • condensation • evaporation • precipitation • run-off • wind |

2 Use these words to complete the description of the water cycle.

| • air • clouds • condensation • cools • evaporation • formed |
| • heated • precipitation • rivers • run-off • snow • water |

1 When the _____ on the earth's surface is _____ by the sun, it turns into water vapour which rises into the _____. This is called _____.

2 Clouds are _____ from water vapour, which _____ as it rises, turning into tiny drops of liquid water. This is called _____.

3 _____ are blown inland by the wind.

4 Clouds get heavy and water falls back to the earth as rain or _____. This is called _____.

5 The water from rain and melted snow is taken by _____ back to the sea. This is called _____.
   The cycle starts again.

18 Cambridge Global English Stage 8 Workbook

3: Rivers and coasts

3 Join the two sentences using *who* or *which*.

1. Marco Polo wrote a book about his travels in central Asia and China. He was born in Venice.
   Marco Polo, who was born in Venice, wrote a book about his travels in central Asia and China.

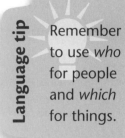

Language tip: Remember to use *who* for people and *which* for things.

2. The Galápagos Islands are part of Ecuador. They are in the Pacific Ocean.

3. Jaguars are good swimmers. They live in South and Central America.

4. Nelson Mandela was the first black president of South Africa. He spent over 27 years in prison.

5. Ahmad ibn Fadlan wrote one of the earliest accounts of the Vikings. He was a famous tenth-century traveller.

6. The Turin Papyrus Map is thought to be the oldest map of Egypt. It is drawn on papyrus.

7. Tutankhamun ruled from about 1336 to 1327 BCE. He is the most famous of the Egyptian pharaohs.

4 In your notebook, write an account of a school trip to an outdoor activity centre using these notes. Use *which* where you can. Start like this:

Last week we went on a school trip to an outdoor activity centre, which was very exciting.

Last week – school trip to an outdoor activity centre – very exciting.
Went whitewater rafting – quite scary.
Boats – for about six people – travelled really fast down the river.
Water – not very deep – extremely cold. Didn't want to fall in!
Went over a small waterfall – a bit of a surprise!
Instructor encouraged us – made us feel more confident.
Hot chocolate and cake after trip – very nice!

Cambridge Global English Stage 8 Workbook

Saved by the bell!

1 The text below is from Unit 3 in your Coursebook. Read it again and find the words for the following.

1. a shaking movement _____
2. an area of calm water next to the land where boats are safe _____
3. moving quickly up and down _____
4. inhabitants of an island _____
5. moved quickly and with a lot of force _____
6. badly damaged, broken into pieces, so they could not be repaired _____

At 6 am on Saturday 27th February 2010, in San Juan Bautista, the island's only town, 12-year-old Martina Maturana felt an earth tremor. She looked out of the window and noticed that the fishing boats in the harbour were bobbing up and down and <u>crashing</u> into each other. She immediately ran 400 metres from her home to the town square to ring the emergency bell. It was Martina's quick thinking which saved the lives of the majority of the 650 islanders. People ran to high ground for safety, escaping the massive wave that was caused by an earthquake off the coast of Chile. A few minutes later, a wall of water crashed onto the land and swept 300 metres into the village. The houses and buildings on the island that were close to the coast were immediately destroyed, including the school at which Martina was a student. "The wave was 20 metres high," said one man whose house was destroyed by the sea. "It was terrifying."

2 Look carefully at the style of the article.

1. Underline words and phrases in the text which the journalist uses to add drama to the account. The first one is done for you: <u>crashing</u>.
2. What information does the journalist give you in the first sentence?
   time, …
3. The journalist uses quite a lot of numbers in the article. Why?

4. Why do you think the journalist ends by quoting the man whose house was destroyed by the sea?

3 Write questions for these answers.

1 Q <u>When did the tsunami hit San Juan Bautista?</u>
   A At 6 am on Saturday 27th February 2010.
2 Q _____
   A 12.
3 Q _____
   A 400 metres.
4 Q _____
   A 650.
5 Q _____
   A 300 metres.
6 Q _____
   A 20 metres.

4 Join each pair of sentences using *which/that* or *who*.

1 What's the name of the island? It was hit by a tsunami in 2010.
<u>What's the name of the island that was hit by a tsunami in 2010?</u>

2 The Juan Fernández Archipelago is a group of islands. They're off the coast of Chile.

3 Juan Fernández was a Spanish sea captain. He was the first to land on the islands in 1574.

4 Alexander Selkirk was a sailor. He was left on one of the islands by the captain of his ship in 1704.

Robinson Crusoe

5 The writer Daniel Defoe wrote a story. The story was based on Alexander Selkirk's experience of living alone on Juan Fernández Island for four years and four months.

6 Juan Fernández was the island. It was renamed Robinson Crusoe Island in 1966.

7 In the story, Robinson Crusoe meets a man on the island. The man becomes his friend.

8 *Robinson Crusoe* is a book. It became one of the most popular children's stories of all time.

4 Great expeditions

Titanic

1 Circle the correct meaning of the word in bold in each sentence.

1 The **wreck** of the *Titanic*, which had sunk in April 1912, was found off the coast of Newfoundland, Canada.
   a the main part of a boat or ship
   b a ship that has been damaged and has sunk to the sea bed
   c the valuable things being carried on a ship

2 In 1986, a three-person **submersible** went down to the wreck, to explore it.
   a an inflatable lifeboat
   b a large scuba-diving suit
   c a small vehicle that can go down very deep in the ocean

3 Since then, there have been several **expeditions** which have brought back 6000 objects.
   a sales of special items
   b short sailing trips
   c organised long journeys which have a particular purpose

4 My great-great-grandfather died when the ship went down, so the ship is really his **grave**.
   a a serious place
   b a place where a dead body is buried
   c a special possession

5 Two people recently went down in a submersible and had their wedding on the **deck** of the *Titanic*.
   a the wide, flat part of a boat or ship on which you can walk around
   b the bottom of a ship or boat
   c a special cabin

2 Circle the correct options.

In 1895, Mary Kingsley ¹*arrived / has arrived* alone on the west coast of Africa. Her plan was to travel up the Ogooué River into Gabon. She ²*has studied / had studied* Zoology and Anthropology and she ³*wanted / has wanted* to study nature and the way people lived in that part of the world.

On June 5th, she ⁴*left / was leaving* the port of Glass in a French steamboat, the *Mové*, and travelled 210 kilometres up-river to

Mary Kingsley

22 Cambridge Global English Stage 8 Workbook

the settlement of Lambaréné. Here she ⁵*was taking / took* another steamboat and travelled further into Gabon. From Ndjole, she continued her journey by canoe because passenger boats ⁶*didn't go / haven't gone* further than Ndjole.

Sometimes, as she ⁷*has travelled / was travelling* up the river, she ⁸*stopped / was stopping* to collect samples of fish. She brought back 65 different types of fish. Three of them ⁹*named / were named* after her. She reached the area where the Fang tribe lived and ¹⁰*was writing / wrote* about them in her book.

Mary Kingsley went to parts of Africa where no-one ¹¹*ever saw / had ever seen* a European woman before. The African women were surprised that a woman ¹²*was travelling / has travelled* without a man. She ¹³*was often asked / was often asking* why she was travelling alone.

Her book, *Travels in Africa*, ¹⁴*published / was published* in 1897. It ¹⁵*has never been / had never been* out of print since that time.

3 Use the text in Exercise 2 to write the questions for these answers.

1 **Q** *Where did Mary Kingsley go in 1895?*
   A To the west coast of Africa.

2 **Q** _____ before she went on her expedition?
   A Zoology and Anthropology.

3 **Q** _____?
   A To travel up the Ogooué River.

4 **Q** _____?
   A Nature and the way people lived in that part of the world.

5 **Q** _____?
   A By steamboat and then by canoe.

6 **Q** _____?
   A 65.

7 **Q** _____?
   A Because she was alone, without a man.

8 **Q** _____?
   A In 1897.

The Treasure Fleet

1 These are the goods that were traded by the Chinese Treasure Fleet. What are they?

1

porcelain

2

s _ _ _

3

w _ _ _

4

i _ _ _ _ y

5

s p _ _ _ _ _

6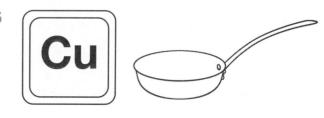

c _ p p _ _

7

j _ w _ _ _

8

p _ _ _ _ _ _

2 Use each of the words in Exercise 1 and the phrases in the box to make true statements.

| • can be used | • is / are used | • was / were used |

1 <u>Porcelain can be used to make cups and bowls.</u>
2 _____
3 _____
4 _____
5 _____
6 _____
7 _____
8 _____

24 Cambridge Global English Stage 8 Workbook

4: Great expeditions

3 Match the words to the definitions.

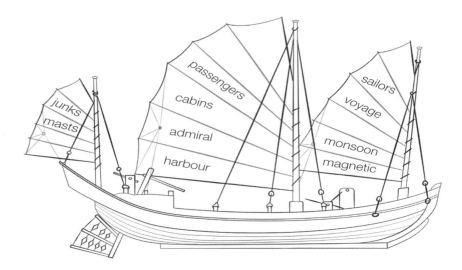

1 A journey by sea. _____
2 The people who work on a ship. _____
3 Rooms to sleep in on a ship. _____
4 A safe place for ships and boats. _____
5 Traditional Chinese sailing boats. _____
6 A type of compass invented long ago in China. _____
7 A type of wind that causes storms of heavy rain in India and South-East Asia. _____
8 The person who is in control of a fleet of ships. _____
9 The people who travel on a ship, but aren't members of the crew. _____
10 The sails of ships are attached to these. _____

4 Use the words from Exercise 3 to complete the text.

In 1402, Zhu Di, the third emperor in the Ming Dynasty, came to power in China. He decided to build a treasure fleet of [1]_____. They were gigantic ships with four [2]_____ and nine sails. Each one carried a crew of more than 200 [3]_____. There was plenty of room for the large crew and there were luxurious [4]_____ with windows and balconies for important [5]_____.

The emperor chose Zheng He to be the [6]_____ of the fleet. By the autumn of 1405, everything was ready and the fleet sailed from Nanjing [7]_____, down the Yangtze river and into the East China Sea.

They sailed 650 kilometres down the coast. They waited at Taiping for favourable [8]_____ winds to take them over the South China Sea to Champa.

The fleet used a [9]_____ compass to find their way when they couldn't see land. The compass had been invented in China over a thousand years before, in about 200 BCE.

Zheng He had been away for almost two years when he finally brought his ship safely home to Nanjing. The [10]_____ had been a great success.

Should we continue to explore space?

1 Solve the crossword.

Across

5 A machine that can move and do some of the work of a person. (5)
6 Where we all live. (5)
10 Journeying to a place to find out about it. (11)
11 Space _____ is going into space for pleasure. (7)

Down

1 A vehicle used for travelling into space. (6)
2 *With 7 Down.* The sun and the very large round objects that move around it. (5, 6)
3 Very large round objects that move around the sun or another star. (7)
4 A space _____ is a place where people can live in space (7)
7 *See 2 Down.*
8 You can see it in the sky at night. (4)
9 The name of one of *3 Down*. (4)

4: Great expeditions

2 Write captions for pictures a to d with words from the crossword.

a _____   c _____
b _____   d _____

3 Complete the sentences using *will/won't* with an appropriate verb.

1 Bye for now. ___I'll see___ you later.
2 You haven't done enough revision. _____ well in the exam.
3 We're getting the 7.30 train, so _____ home at 8 o'clock.
4 The sky's really clear tonight. _____ a nice day tomorrow.
5 _____ me a text to let me know you've arrived safely?
6 Thanks very much, but _____ for dinner. I've got to go.
7 He's been training really hard, so I think _____ well in the match on Saturday.
8 Don't worry about buying anything on the way home. _____ enough for everyone.

4 Rewrite these statements using the passive with *will*. Use *by* where necessary.

1 Electricity will power cars and other vehicles.
2 Robots will build all machines.
3 Solar farms and wind turbines will generate electricity.
4 Computers will control cars.
5 Teachers will give lessons over the Internet.
6 We'll make all calls on mobile phones, not landlines.
7 A team from Africa will win the World Cup.
8 People from Earth will inhabit Mars.

1 _Cars and other vehicles will be powered by electricity._
2 _____
3 _____
4 _____
5 _____
6 _____
7 _____
8 _____

Cambridge Global English Stage 8 Workbook

5 Sports and hobbies

Sport for all

1 Solve the crossword.

13

1

11

Across
4 In this sport, the scoring goes 0, 15, 30, 40, … . (6)
6 You play this outside with a bat and a red ball. (7)
8 An American game in which a pitcher throws a ball to a batter. (8)
10 You play this outside with a small ball which you hit a long way. (4)
11 You travel down snow-covered mountains. (6)
13 See picture 13.
14 In American English, this sport is called 'soccer'. (8)

Down
1 See picture 1.
2 This type of sport includes running, high jump and long jump. (9)
3 You score points by throwing a ball into a basket. (10)
5 Moving through water in a pool, for example. (8)
6 You need two wheels for this. (7)
7 You do it on snow with a big board. (12)
9 You can play this on the beach. (10)
11 See picture 11.
12 You run with the ball in your hands and you can kick it. (5)

5: Sports and hobbies

2 Complete the sentences with the correct words. Then name the sport.

| • cap | • gloves | • goggles | • javelin | • lane | • puck |
| • reins | • rider | • saddle | • skates | • stumps | |

1. Sit down in the ___saddle___ and don't hold the _____ too tightly. That's good. You'll make a good _____.
   sport: _horse riding_

2. I've got my own _____ now. They're really comfortable. I can do a figure of eight without falling over.
   sport: _____

3. Now, when you get into the ring, remember to hold your hands up, so that your _____ protect your face.
   sport: _____

4. I train every morning. I go up and down the fast _____ in the pool. I always wear a _____ and goggles.
   sport: _____

5. I rent my skis and poles, but I've got my own _____. You need them when the sun's bright or when it's snowing.
   sport: _____

6. It's a game of great skill. You use your stick to hit the _____ and to carry it as well. You have to be able to skate really well too.
   sport: _____

7. I enjoy running, throwing the _____ and doing the high jump.
   sport: _____

8. In this game, the bowler tries to hit the _____, which are behind the batsman.
   sport: _____

3 Use the words from the two columns to make compound nouns. Then label the pictures.

1 _____

2 _____

3 _____

4 _____

5 _____

6 _____

7 _____

boxing	pad
elbow	riding
high	post
ice	ring
horse	pad
goal	jump
knee	skating

Cambridge Global English Stage 8 Workbook

At the top of their game

1 Read the text and choose the correct answers.

In recent years, many of Barcelona Football Club's best players have come from the club's youth academy, La Masía. Talented youngsters are chosen from all over Spain and from other countries to live and train at the academy. Lionel Messi, for example, moved there from his home in Argentina when he was only 13. Living and training together helps the boys to develop the team spirit that is so important in a team sport.

The young players must have natural talent, good co–ordination, speed and agility. They also need an instinctive ability to make quick decisions on the pitch.

1 What is La Masía?
   a It's a town.
   b It's a football school.
   c It's football club.
2 The students at La Masía are from
   a Spain.
   b Spain and Argentina.
   c several different countries.
3 The boys at La Masía
   a go home at the end of each day.
   b sleep there as well as train there.
   c go there just to play football.
4 Lionel Messi is
   a Spanish.
   b Argentinian.
   c from Barcelona.
5 The boys are encouraged to
   a learn to play together well.
   b think of themselves first.
   c think carefully about every move they make.

30 Cambridge Global English Stage 8 Workbook

5: Sports and hobbies

2 Match the words in the columns to make collocations connected with sport.

1	hand–eye	talent	1 _____
2	powers of	spirit	2 _____
3	steely	concentration	3 _____
4	team	co–ordination	4 _____
5	natural	determination	5 _____

3 Think of the sports you play. Write a sentence about your strong points and the things you'd like to improve on.

I've got (quite good) …, but I need to improve my … .

_____

4 Use these abstract nouns to complete the sentences. Add *the* where necessary.

• ability   • ambition   • co–ordination   • determination   • flexibility   • speed

1 In a sport like ice hockey, _co–ordination_ is very important because you need to skate and hit the puck into a small goal.
2 It's _____ of many young athletes to compete in the Olympic Games.
3 Ballet dancers and gymnasts need to have a lot of _____ in their bodies.
4 Sprinters need _____ but marathon runners need to be able to keep going over a long distance.
5 Good footballers and rugby players have _____ to make quick decisions on the pitch.
6 In order to be top in your sport, you need to have _____ to succeed.

5 Underline the stressed syllables in these words:

1 agility
2 activity
3 creativity
4 imagination
5 participation
6 competition

Pronunciation: Word stress

It's important to know where the stress falls in longer words. When you note down a new word, underline the syllable where the main stress falls. You will start to notice patterns:

a<u>bi</u>lity   co–ordi<u>na</u>tion
flexi<u>bi</u>lity   determi<u>na</u>tion
am<u>bi</u>tion   concent<u>ra</u>tion

Study skills

What are your hobbies?

1 _____

2 _____

3 _____

4 _____

5 _____

6 _____

7 _____

8 _____

9 _____

1 Write a caption for each picture. Choose from the following phrases and the words in the box.

He/She likes
     enjoys
He's/She's into
     keen on
His/Her hobby is

- acting
- doing karate
- making models
- trampolining
- collecting coins
- drawing
- playing the drums
- writing stories
- collecting shells
- juggling
- playing the guitar
- making jewellery
- singing

5: Sports and hobbies

> **Language tip**
>
> **for** and **since**
>
> Remember to use *for* when you give the length of time:
>
> *I've been playing table tennis for seven years.*
>
> Use *since* when you give the start of a time:
>
> *I've been playing table tennis since I was 5 years old.*
>
> *I've been playing the guitar since 10 o'clock this morning.*
>
> *I've been learning the guitar since 2010.*

2 Write questions using *How long* and the present perfect continuous. Write answers using *for* and *since*.

1 **Q** you / collect shells? **Q** How long have you been collecting shells?
  A three years **A** For three years.

2 **Q** you / play the drums? **Q** _____
  A 10 years old **A** Since I …

3 **Q** your brother / make model cars? **Q** _____
  A five years **A** _____

4 **Q** your sister / write stories? **Q** _____
  A 7 years old **A** _____

5 **Q** you / do karate? **Q** _____
  A two years **A** _____

3 Choose a verb to complete the sentences using the present perfect continuous.

• collect • do (x2) • learn • make • play (x2) • wait

1 I'm really tired. I _____ judo for two hours.
2 Sorry I'm late. I _____ tennis.
3 We _____ coins for seven years.
4 My brother _____ the drums for an hour.
5 Come on! We _____ for you for half an hour.
6 We _____ jewellery to give as presents.
7 I _____ to ride a horse, but I've fallen off quite a lot.
8 What _____ you _____? You're covered in paint.

Cambridge Global English Stage 8 Workbook

6 Entertainment and media

What are you into?

1 Use suitable words to complete what Lucia, Ramesh and Amil are saying.

I've taken up the flute. I'm [1]_____ into it. I absolutely love it. [2]_____ went to this amazing concert. It [3]_____ so cool! You say you don't [4]_____ classical music, but you should give [5]_____ a try.

I do taekwondo, which is a [6]_____ art that helps you develop strength, [7]_____, balance and agility. I prefer doing [8]_____ to doing team sports, like football.

[9]_____ my taekwondo class I am usually [10]_____ tired, so I stay in and [11]_____ to some music to relax.

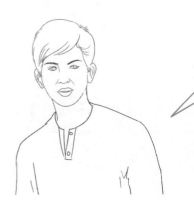

I've been playing chess since I [12]_____ four years old. I really enjoy [13]_____. I started playing with my dad [14]_____ now I'm in the chess club [15]_____ school. We go to competitions all [16]_____ the country. I often play against [17]_____ much older than me and I [18]_____ win! You need good powers of [19]_____ for chess and you need determination [20]_____ well.

6: Entertainment and media

2 Write five sentences that are true for you using the words in the table below.

1 enjoy	play	music
2 prefer	do	the flute / piano / guitar / …
3 love	go	swimming
4 don't mind	go out	football / volleyball / …
5 (don't) like	listen to	martial arts / karate / judo / taekwondo
	watch	to the cinema / a restaurant / a concert
		with friends / with my family
		video games
		TV

I enjoy going out with friends.

1 _____
2 _____
3 _____
4 _____
5 _____

3 Complete the phrasal verbs in these sentences.

1 Would you like to come _round_ to my house on Saturday to watch TV?
2 I gave _____ judo because I didn't have time to do it.
3 We've been working really hard this week, so let's just stay _____ and chill _____ this evening.
4 My friend's taken _____ riding. He loves horses.
5 I'm going _____ with my aunt and uncle at the weekend.
6 My dad and my brother are really _____ cars. They always watch the Grand Prix races on TV.

Study skills

Learning phrasal verbs

To help you remember phrasal verbs, think of an example which means something to you personally and write it down.

I**'m into** martial arts.

My cousins often **come round** at the weekend and we **chill out**.

I want to **take up** karate next year.

4 Write three sentences about yourself using some of the phrasal verbs in Exercise 3.

_____
_____
_____

At the circus

1 Read the text and find:

1 The name of a country
_____

2 Two words to describe people who watch a circus performance
_____   _____

3 A word for people who take part in a circus
_____

4 Four sports
_____   _____   _____   _____

> The Cirque du Soleil is a circus from Quebec in Canada. It has given performances to 100 million spectators in more than 300 cities in over forty countries on six continents.
>
> About half of Cirque du Soleil's 1300 performers are athletes who have trained in gymnastics, trampolining, swimming and diving. Some of them have even competed at the Olympics. The Cirque du Soleil amazes audiences around the world. They are part acrobatic circus, part theatre with a little extra magic. The one thing the Cirque du Soleil doesn't have is animals.
>
> They think it's wrong to use animals in circuses. They do not agree with the way animals are trained. "They are animals, not performers. They should be in the jungle," says one of the troupe's directors. "We will never have animals in our shows."

2 Write questions for these answers using the information in the text in Exercise 1.

1 **Q** _____
   A Quebec, in Canada.

2 **Q** _____
   A 1300.

3 **Q** _____
   A Animals.

4 **Q** _____
   A Because they don't agree with the way animals are trained.

6: Entertainment and media

3 Complete the sentences by putting the words in brackets in the correct order.

1 I _____ the Cirque du Soleil (*seen / just / have*).
2 It _____ the best circus I _____. (*definitely / is*) (*ever / have / seen*)
3 They _____ animals in their circuses. (*use / never*)
4 My friend _____ it twice and she's going again next week. (*already / seen / has*)
5 You _____ a ticket to see the circus if you book straightaway. (*probably / get / can*)

4 Solve the crossword.

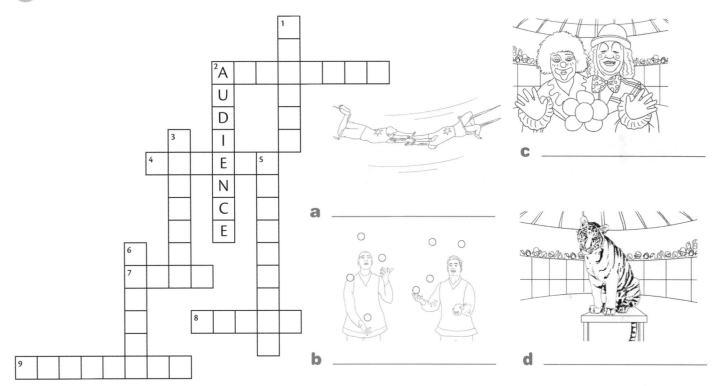

Across

2 Gymnasts who perform in a circus. (8)
4 *1 Down* wear this on their faces. (4, 2)
7 The circus _____ is where the circus takes place. (4)
8 A big striped cat that sometimes appears at a circus. (5)
9 They keep three or more objects moving through the air by throwing and catching them quickly. (8)

Down

1 They wear funny clothes and make people laugh at a circus. (6)
2 The people who watch a circus, a play or a film. (8)
3 A vehicle in which circus performers live when they are on tour. (7)
5 Another word for entertainer. (9)
6 A group of circus performers. (6)

5 Write a caption for each circus picture using words from the crossword.

A film review

1 Read the film review. What does each paragraph do?

Paragraph
1. gives an opinion of the script and the film techniques
2. gives an overall opinion
3. gives examples of good points about the film
4. introduces the film
5. summarises the plot

Toy Story 3

Movie	Toy Story 3
Director	Lee Unkrich
Voiced By	Tom Hanks
	Tim Allen

1. What's the best family film of all time? It's difficult to choose, but the *Toy Story* series would certainly be in the top ten. And if I had to choose one, it would be *Toy Story 3*. This 3D computer-animated comedy drama is directed by Lee Unkrich and stars Woody, voiced by Tom Hanks, and Buzz Lightyear, voiced by Tim Allen. Several other well-known actors' voices are used for other characters. The story is set in a town in America.

2. At the beginning of the film, Andy, 17, is leaving for college. He's clearing his room for his little sister. He decides to take Woody with him to college and he leaves the other toys to be put in a room at the top of the house. However, the toys are sent to a children's play centre by mistake, where they have a very difficult time. Woody comes to the rescue and the toys are finally taken in by a girl called Bonnie, who gives them a good home.

As you watch the film, you have no idea of the terrible things that are going to happen to the toys. This is part of the film's success because you are kept in suspense: you really don't know whether the toys are going to survive. However, the film ends happily and there are some very funny moments, such as when Buzz is reprogrammed and starts speaking Spanish.

The script is well written and the CGI (computer-generated imagery) is amazing. The soundtrack includes songs such as *We Belong Together* and *You've got a Friend in Me*.

This is a truly wonderful film for all the family. I thoroughly recommend it.

2 Answer the questions.

1 How does the film create suspense?
_____

2 How does the film end?
_____

3 Is there humour in the film? Give an example.
_____

4 On a star rating of 1 to 5, where 1 is 'very bad' and 5 is 'excellent', how many stars do you think this reviewer would give the film?
_____

3 Use the notes to write the first paragraph of a review about *Finding Nemo*. Look at the review of *Toy Story* 3 to help you. If you've seen *Finding Nemo*, add your opinions of it.

Film title: *Finding Nemo*	Voices: Albert Brooks (Marlin), Alexander Gould (Nemo)
Type of film: 3D computer-animated comedy adventure film	Location: the Pacific Ocean off the east coast of Australia, including the Great Barrier Reef and Sydney Harbour
Writer and director: Andrew Stanton	
Main characters: a fish called Marlin who searches for his lost son, Nemo	Suitable for: adults and children

<u>Finding Nemo is …</u> (continue in your notebook)

4 Which phrases in the review in Exercise 1 could you use in a review of another film?
_____
_____
_____

How would you adapt the phrases to use in the review of a book?
_____
_____
_____

Study skills

Using a model to improve your writing

When you're writing in a particular style (for example, an informal email, a formal letter, a review, an advert), try to follow a model text as closely as possible. That way, you'll learn certain phrases that you can use in the future.

7 Household routines

In the kitchen

1 Complete the words.

1 d _ _ _ w _ _ _ _ r
2 o _ _ n
3 t _ _ p _ t
4 s _ _ _ _ p _ n
5 f r _ _ _ e
6 f r _ _ _ _ r
7 s c _ _ _ s
8 m _ _ _ _ w _ _ e
9 i _ _ n
10 c _ _ _ _ e m _ _ _ _ _ e
11 w _ _ _ _ _ g m _ _ _ _ _ e
12 t _ n o _ _ _ _ r
13 f _ y _ _ g p _ n
14 f _ _ e ex _ _ _ _ _ _ _ _ _ r

2 Find the words on the fridge to match the definitions. (Clue: they're all compound nouns.)

1 You iron your clothes on it. _____

2 You use it to change channels on the TV.
_____

3 It takes away steam and smells from the kitchen.
_____

4 It's a machine that helps you to prepare food.
_____

5 You use it to turn the light on and off.
_____

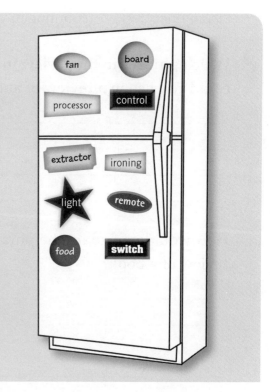

Cambridge Global English Stage 8 Workbook

3 Use the phrasal verbs from the Study skills box in these sentences. Remember to put the verbs in the correct form.

A bad day

Yesterday morning, I ¹ __woke up__ early. I ² _____ _____ the light and saw it was only 5.30, so I went back to sleep. The next thing I knew, it was 8.00. So I ³ _____ _____ very quickly, I ⁴ _____ _____ my school clothes and I ran to the bus stop. I ⁵ _____ _____ the first bus that came. But it was the wrong bus, so I ⁶ _____ _____ at the next stop and ran all the way to school. My teacher ⁷ _____ me _____ for being late. I tried to explain, but she just told me to ⁸ _____ _____ at my desk and be quiet.

After school, I decided to walk home with my friends. We sat on a bench in the park. I ⁹ _____ my mobile phone _____ on the bench and we chatted. When we left, I forgot to ¹⁰ _____ it _____. I only realised when I got home that I'd left it in the park, so I had to run back to find it. Luckily it was still there.

I went home. I was feeling tired, so I thought, "I'll ¹¹ _____ _____ for half an hour before supper". I ¹² _____ _____ my jacket and I lay on the bed. Then Mum came into my room and said, "Dad and I ¹³ _____ _____ _____ at a restaurant tonight. Your supper's cooking in the oven. The dishwasher's broken, so make sure you ¹⁴ _____ _____ and ¹⁵ _____ the dishes _____. Oh, and don't disturb Tanya. She's in her room revising for an exam." I thought, "Great, Mum. Thanks a lot!"

Anyway, guess what? I fell asleep and when I woke up my supper was burnt, so I had to ¹⁶ _____ it _____. That was a bad day.

Phrasal verbs

Phrasal verbs are very common in English. Using them correctly shows that you have a good command of the language.

eat out	sit down
get off	stand up
get on	take off
get up	tell off
lie down	throw away
pick up	turn off
put away	turn on
put down	wake up
put on	wash up

In my room

1 Solve the crossword.

Across

5 You can keep your books on these. (11)
7 Area you can stand or sit on outside an upstairs window or door. (7)
11 One wall is papered, but the others are _____ white. (7)
12 A cover for a bed. (9)
13 If you win a race, you may get a gold one. (5)

Down

1 Prizes you get for winning a race or a competition. (8)
2 The part of your life when you are a child. (9)
3 A group of similar objects that someone has put together. (10)
4 Untidy. (5)
5 You sleep on them; they are fixed together with one on top of the other. (4, 4)
6 A piece of furniture in which you hang up your clothes. (8)
8 You can keep things in this piece of furniture which has doors and sometimes shelves. (8)
9 The opposite of *4 Down*. (4)
10 Teddy bears are soft _____. (4)

7: Household routines

2 Complete each sentence with a suitable verb in the correct form. Here are some verbs to help you.

• add • be • get • hang • have • hold • keep • put • save • stack • stay • win

1 I like bright colours, but I'<u>m</u> not keen on lime green.
2 I'm going to decorate my bedroom and I'm going to _____ lots of pictures up on the walls.
3 If my sister _____ her own way, she'd have pink walls and a sky blue ceiling.
4 I like posters on my walls because they _____ colour and interest to the room.
5 I have to tidy my room when it _____ really messy.
6 I've got a very big wardrobe. It _____ all my clothes.
7 My brother has _____ a lot of medals for swimming, including a gold one.
8 I try to _____ my room tidy, but after my little cousins have been in it, it's a real mess.
9 That's amazing! Your clothes are all _____ neatly in your wardrobe.
10 I haven't got enough room on my bookshelves, so I _____ my books on the floor.
11 My mum threw out my collection of football magazines. But I went to the bin and I managed to _____ them.
12 I don't want to change my bedroom. I want it to _____ as it is.

3 Think of something in each of these colours and write a sentence about it.

• lime green • light blue • dark blue • bright red • apple green
• olive green • jet black • snow white • chocolate brown

1 <u>We've got a lime green bin at home.</u>
2 _____
3 _____
4 _____
5 _____
6 _____
7 _____
8 _____
9 _____

4 Write a list of ten things you've got in your bedroom.

_____
_____
_____

Cambridge Global English Stage 8 Workbook

Jobs at home

1 Write answers to these questions.

1 How often do you tidy your room?
   _____

2 How would you describe your room?
   _____
   _____

3 Do you always make your own bed? How often?
   _____

4 Do you ever put the rubbish out? How often?
   _____

5 Who sets the table? Who clears the table? Do you ever help?
   _____
   _____

6 Who does the washing up? Do you ever help?
   _____

7 Do you ever clean the bathroom? How often?
   _____

8 Could you prepare dinner? What would you make?
   _____
   _____

9 Do you know how to iron a shirt? Which part of the shirt do you start with? What do you do next?
   _____
   _____

10 What would you do if a button had come off your school shirt?
   _____
   _____

7: Household routines

2 Write sentences comparing the two things.

my room (3 metres square) / your room (5 metres square).
(small)
My room _is much smaller than your room._
OR
My room _is far smaller than your room._
my room (3 metres square) / your room (5 metres square).
(big)
My room _is nowhere near as big as your room._
my room (lime green and sky blue) / your room (bright red and orange).
(colourful)
My room _is just as colourful as your room._

1 Rob Stewart (15 goals this season) / Ryan Jones (15 goals this season)
  (good at football).
  Rob Stewart _____

2 Sara (100 metres in 15 seconds) / Rosanna (100 metres in 25 seconds)
  (fast)
  Sara _____
  Rosanna _____

3 Tom (1 m 80) / Callum (1 m 80)
  (tall)
  Tom _____

4 the Acme dishwasher (£750) / the Zenith dishwasher (£350)
  (expensive)
  The Acme _____
  The Zenith _____

5 the saucepan (500 g) / the frying pan (3 kg)
  (heavy)
  The saucepan _____
  The frying pan _____

6 a microwave (60 seconds to heat up a bowl of soup) / a fan oven (15 minutes)
  (quick)
  A microwave _____
  A fan oven _____

Cambridge Global English Stage 8 Workbook

8 Habitat interactions

Rainforests

1 Match the two halves of each sentence.

1. Tropical rainforests cover
2. The Amazon in South America is
3. Tropical rainforests are home to
4. The plants provide
5. More than 25% of our modern medicines
6. And there are many more medicines

a. food and shelter for the many animals that live there.
b. come from tropical forest plants.
c. over 30 million types of plants and animals.
d. the largest tropical rainforest in the world.
e. yet to be discovered.
f. about 8% of the world's land surface.

2 Read the definitions and write the scientific words.

1. The process by which a plant makes its own food. (This only happens during daylight.)

   _____

2. A gas that is produced when people and animals breathe out, or when carbon is burned.

   _____

3. A gas that is in the air and that people and animals need to live.

   _____

4. A type of sugar produced in plants.

   _____

3 Use the words from the box to complete the text.

| • carbon dioxide | • glucose | • leaves | • oxygen |
| • photosynthesis | • roots | • sunlight | |

The word [1]_____ means 'putting together by light'. It is the process by which plants make their food. This is how it works. Plants get energy from [2]_____. They take in [3]_____ from the air through their [4]_____ and they take up water from the ground through their [5]_____. The plants use the energy to turn the water and the carbon dioxide into [6]_____. As part of this process, the plants also release [7]_____ into the air.

4 Complete the text using the present passive of the verbs in brackets.

It (think) [1] _is thought_ that more than half the earth's rainwater (hold) [2]_____ by the Amazon forests. Water (take up) [3]_____ by the forest trees. It (release) [4]_____ into the atmosphere. Mist and clouds (form) [5]_____.

Rainforests are sometimes called 'the lungs of the earth'. They help to keep the air clean and to provide the oxygen we need to breathe. During photosynthesis, carbon dioxide (take in) [6]_____ by the trees and oxygen (give out) [7]_____.

5 Write the sentences in the correct places.

Carbon dioxide is taken in and oxygen is given out.
Neither oxygen nor carbon dioxide are given out or taken in.
The plant produces more carbon dioxide than oxygen.
More oxygen than carbon dioxide is produced.

There is no photosynthesis.
When it's dark, oxygen is taken in and carbon dioxide is given out.
~~When there is bright light, photosynthesis happens.~~
When there is dim light, both photosynthesis and respiration take place.

1 _When there is bright light, photosynthesis happens._
2 _____
3 _____
4 _____
5 _____
6 _____
7 _____
8 _____

Live and let live

1 Read the article below to find out more about Richard Turere and his lion lights. Which paragraph relates to the diagram?

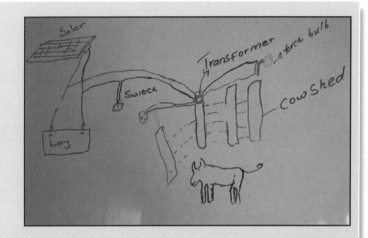

Before he invented the lion lights, Richard tried other ways of protecting the cows from the lions. His first idea was to use fire because he thought lions were afraid of fire. However, he soon realised that it didn't work. In fact, it had the opposite effect. It helped the lions to see the cattle in the cowshed. His next idea was to make a scarecrow to make the lions think that someone was there all the time to protect the animals. But lions are clever. They realised the scarecrow wasn't a real person because it didn't move. Then, one night, when he was walking around the cowshed with a torch, he discovered that the lions were scared of a moving light. He realised that they connected moving lights with people. That was when he had the idea for his lion lights.

He used a solar panel to produce electricity and he connected it to an old car battery, which stored the electricity. He found an old indicator box from a motorcycle and he connected this to the battery. He also connected the indicator box, which he called a 'transformer', to the bulb from an old torch. The indicator box made the lights flash on and off, just as the indicators on a car flash to show a change of direction. The flashing lights made the lions think that someone was walking around the cowshed protecting the animals, so they stayed away.

Since Richard has set up the lion lights at his parents' farm, none of the family's cattle have been attacked by lions. The lights have also been used by other farmers around Kenya with the same success.

Understanding meaning from context

Find these words in the text in Exercise 1:
cowshed   scarecrow   battery   indicators

We know that:
- fire helped the lions see the cattle in the cowshed.
- Richard walked around the cowshed with a torch.

So a *cowshed* is a place where cows are kept.

2 Try to work out the meaning of these words: a scarecrow, a battery, indicators.

8: Habitat interactions

3 Look at the magazine article in Exercise 1 again and answer the questions.

1. How did Richard try to protect the animals before he invented the lion lights?
   _____
2. Why didn't Richard's first idea work?
   _____
3. What is the word for cows kept on a farm?
   _____
4. Why didn't Richard's second idea work?
   _____
5. Why did his third idea work?
   _____
6. Why did Richard need an old car battery?
   _____
7. Why did Richard need an indicator box from a motorbike?
   _____
8. Think of a title for the magazine article.
   _____

4 Complete these notes to give the key facts in the magazine article.

Problem: _____
Richard's first idea: _____
His second idea: _____
His third idea: _____
Materials and devices used: _____
_____
Result: _____
_____

5 Choose the correct form of the present perfect, active or passive, to complete the sentences.

1. Many lions (*kill*) _____ because they (*attack*) _____ cattle and other animals.
2. Richard Turere (*invent*) _____ a device for keeping lions away from farms.
3. The device (*be*) _____ a success for Richard's family.
4. Richard's lion lights (*use*) _____ all over Kenya.
5. Richard (*offer*) _____ a scholarship at one of Kenya's top schools.
6. Richard (*present*) _____ the idea for his lion lights at a conference in California.

Cambridge Global English Stage 8 Workbook

The food chain

1 Solve the crossword.

Across

3. An animal that kills and eats other animals. (8)
5. *See 12 Across.*
6. A scientific word for an animal that eats a plant or another animal. (8)
8. An animal that only eats plants. (9)
10. An animal that is hunted and eaten by another animal. (4)
12. *With 5 Across.* A diagram showing how energy passes from one plant or animal to another. (4, 5)
13. An animal with a very long neck. (7)
14. An insect with colourful wings. (9)

Down

1. A brightly coloured blue and orange bird that lives near water and eats fish. (10)
2. *With 4 Down.* Another name for a puma. (8, 4)
4. *See 2 Down.*
6. An animal that eats other animals. (9)
7. Insects that make honey. (4)
9. A three-dimensional shape with triangular sides. (7)
10. A scientific word for a plant that makes its own food by photosynthesis. (8)
11. A black and white striped animal, like a horse. (5)

8: Habitat interactions

2 Complete the interview with suitable words. (Some of the words are short words like *a/an, the, and*, etc.)

> We know about how grass is ¹_____ by animals and they're eaten by ²_____ animals. But can the food chain ³_____ wrong?
>
> Yes, that can happen. Keeping ⁴_____ balance right in the food chain ⁵_____ very important. In some parts of ⁶_____ world, the number of plants, trees ⁷_____ flowers has been dramatically reduced ⁸_____ human activity.
>
> **What do you mean exactly?**
>
> ⁹_____ have been cut down for wood. Buildings ¹⁰_____ been put on land where ¹¹_____ was once grass and flowers.
>
> **And ¹²_____ is the effect of that?**
>
> It means that ¹³_____ aren't as many plants for the ¹⁴_____, such as deer, to eat. So ¹⁵_____ deer find it hard to get ¹⁶_____. And their numbers go down. In turn, the ¹⁷_____ at the top of ¹⁸_____ food chain, like mountain lions, have fewer deer to ¹⁹_____, so their numbers ²⁰_____ down as well.
>
> **Does this have ²¹_____ effect on the smaller animals like ²²_____ and insects?**
>
> Yes, it does. It ²³_____ that there aren't as many plants ²⁴_____ flowers for butterflies, bees and other ²⁵_____. So birds like kingfishers have fewer ²⁶_____ to eat and their numbers go ²⁷_____.

3 Give an example of each of the following:

1 a predator   _____
2 a carnivore _____
3 a herbivore _____
4 an omnivore _____

Cambridge Global English Stage 8 Workbook

9 Buildings and structures

Brilliant buildings

1 Write the name of:

1 a building to which you go to see ancient objects   m _____
2 a place where kings and queens live   p _____
3 a very tall, thin structure   t _____
4 a building with triangular sides   p _____
5 a building where you can see a performance involving singing and acting   o _____ h _____
6 a building where you can see sports events   s _____
7 three religious buildings   c _____ , m _____ , t _____

2 Choose a preposition from the box to complete each question.

• in (x4)   • of (x2)   • to (x2)   • from   • over

1 _____ which country is the ancient city of Ur?
2 _____ which country is Rome the capital?
3 _____ which city would you go if you wanted to see the Kremlin?
4 _____ which capital city would you sail down the Nile to see the Pyramids?
5 _____ which city is the Parthenon?
6 _____ which city would you go if you wanted to visit the Louvre museum?
7 _____ which country is the temple of Angkor Wat?
8 _____ which city is there a building with a roof that looks like the sails on a ship?
9 _____ which city are you flying if you can see the River Thames?
10 _____ which country is Kuala Lumpur the capital?

Cambridge Global English Stage 8 Workbook

9: Buildings and structures

3 In the word square, find the answers to the questions in Exercise 2. Write them here.

1 _____   6 _____
2 _____   7 _____
3 _____   8 _____
4 _____   9 _____
5 _____ 10 _____

4 Find the names of three more countries and two more cities in the word square.

Countries

1 _____
2 _____
3 _____

c	a	i	r	o	f	y	u	w	b	g	g
k	e	s	y	d	n	e	y	z	z	u	n
q	s	i	s	t	a	n	b	u	l	u	z
m	e	x	i	c	o	r	i	t	a	l	y
m	v	l	w	o	m	o	s	c	o	w	q
a	j	o	e	m	v	f	z	s	o	c	o
l	s	n	c	a	m	b	o	d	i	a	x
a	o	d	u	x	u	i	n	u	d	n	j
y	j	o	r	d	a	n	i	b	l	a	a
s	w	n	d	i	z	n	r	a	g	d	v
i	p	a	r	i	s	a	a	i	p	a	c
a	a	t	h	e	n	s	q	q	k	i	n

Cities

4 _____
5 _____

5 Choose the correct answer to each question in the quiz.

Quick Quiz

1 What is the Alhambra?
   a a temple   **b** a palace   **c** a pyramid

2 What is the Louvre?
   a a tower   **b** an opera house   **c** a museum

3 What is El Castillo at Chichén Itzá?
   a a pyramid   **b** a palace   **c** a museum

4 What is Petra?
   a an ancient ruined city   **b** an ancient tower   **c** an ancient Greek temple

Art meets engineering

1 Label the bridge with the words and phrases from the box.

• curve • cables • traffic • sloping • pier • pylon

1 _____
2 _____
3 a slight _____
4 gently _____
5 four lanes of _____, two in each direction
6 _____

2 Choose the correct form of the past continuous, active or passive, to complete the sentences.

1 The flight was delayed, so people (tell) _were being told_ to wait in the departure lounge.

2 I (laugh) _____ so much that I fell off my chair.

3 We couldn't use the swimming pool because it (clean) _____ .

4 This photo shows my parents in Miami. They (introduce) _____ to David Beckham!

5 They arrived at the port just as the ferry (leave) _____ .

6 The ball hit my head and the next thing I knew was that I (carry) _____ off the pitch.

7 We didn't know at the time, but our school play (film) _____ for the local TV news.

8 When the new school (build) _____ , the builders found some old Roman coins and jewellery.

9 Mum gave the coffee machine away because it (not / use) _____ .

10 I fell off my bike because I (not / look) _____ where I (go) _____ .

> **Remember**
> Past continuous active:
> They **were building** a bridge.
> Past continuous passive:
> A bridge **was being built**.

54 Cambridge Global English Stage 8 Workbook

9: Buildings and structures

Name	Jiaozhou Bay Bridge	Rio Negro Bridge
Country	China	Brazil
Type of bridge	Suspension and cable-stayed	Cable-stayed
Height	149 metres	55 metres
Length	42 kilometres	3,595 metres
Number of piers	More than 5000	246
Number of traffic lanes	6 (3 in each direction)	4 (2 in each direction)
Time taken to build it	4 years	3 years
Time taken to cross it by car	30 minutes	5 minutes

3 Complete the text about the Jiaozhou Bay Bridge using the information in the chart above.

The Jiaozhou Bay Bridge in [1]_____ is a suspension and [2]_____ bridge. It is [3]_____ high and [4]_____ long. It is supported by more than [5]_____ piers. The deck of the bridge has [6]_____ for traffic, [7]_____ in each direction. In total, the bridge took [8]_____ to build. It takes [9]_____ to cross it by car.

4 Write a similar text about the Rio Negro Bridge.

_____
_____
_____
_____
_____

5 Find out one more fact about each bridge.

The Jiaozhou Bay Bridge _____
_____.

The Rio Negro Bridge _____
_____.

Cambridge Global English Stage 8 Workbook

School design challenge

1 Complete each sentence by using a word from each box to make collocations.

central	natural
air	safety
outdoor play	ground
noise	surrounding
local	open-air

classrooms	floor
conditioning	heating
countryside	levels
environment	light
features	area

1 "Our school doesn't really fit in with the _local environment_ because it's old and all the houses around it are very modern."

2 "We really need _____ _____ in our school because it's very hot in summer."

3 "Our classroom was freezing yesterday because the _____ _____ wasn't working."

4 "All schools, not just primary schools, need an _____ _____. It isn't good to be inside all the time and you need somewhere to play football at break time."

5 "Sometimes it's really hard to concentrate because of the _____ _____ from other classrooms. We need better sound insulation."

6 "It's good to have plenty of _____ _____ because it makes it easier to read and you don't need to have the lights on all the time."

7 "_____ _____, such as fire extinguishers, clearly marked fire exits and self-closing doors are very important in schools."

8 "Our school is three storeys high. All the classrooms are on the first and second floors; the school hall, the dining-room, the gym and the school office are on the _____ _____."

9 "In my ideal school, the classrooms would have big windows looking out over the _____ _____."

10 "I love the idea of having _____ _____, so that you can have lessons outside when the weather's good."

9: Buildings and structures

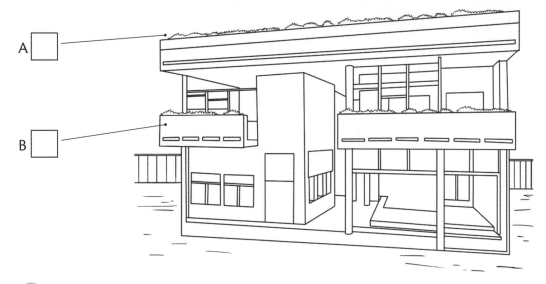

2 Draw lines to match the two halves of each caption. Then find captions for A and B on the picture.

1 A flexible classroom on the ground floor opens onto the street,
2 Outside the classrooms there are balconies
3 The classrooms on the first floor are light,
4 The computer room, which is used as
5 There are cool open-air classrooms
6 Visitors can walk through the school
7 You can sit on the steps and watch a film

an internet café outside school hours, is on the ground floor.
bringing the outside world into the classroom.
but they also have blinds at the windows to provide shade.
on the roof.
on the screen that rolls down on the wall of the internet café.
to see what is happening in the classrooms.
with plants which the students look after.

3 What do you like about the design of the school described in Exercise 2? Is there anything you don't like? Give your opinions here. You can use the phrases in the box to introduce your opinions.

- What I like about this design is that …
- I particularly like …
- However, I think the architect could have …
- I'm not so sure about …

_____
_____
_____

Cambridge Global English Stage 8 Workbook

10 Design and shape

A bar of chocolate

1 Write the items next to the appropriate phrases.

• bananas	• biscuits	• bread	• cake	• cheese	• chocolate	• chocolates	• cola	• crisps
• flour	• flowers	• grapes	• honey	• ice cream	• jam	• matches	• meat	• milk
• olives	• soap	• soup	• sugar	• sweets	• tissues	• toast	• water	• yogurt

1 a bar of _____
2 a loaf of _____
3 a slice of _____
4 a packet of _____
5 a bunch of _____
6 a box of _____
7 a jar of _____
8 a carton of _____
9 a bottle of _____
10 a can of _____
11 a bag of _____
12 a tin of _____

2 Complete the dialogue with the correct words from Exercise 1. Remember to make them plural where necessary.

Mum: Here's the shopping list.
William: Right, bread. How much bread?
Mum: A couple of [1]_____.
William: And meat?
Mum: Oh, just get a few [2]_____ of cold meat.
William: What sort of meat?
Mum: Whatever you like.
William: OK. Biscuits?
Mum: Yes, a [3]_____ of those nice almond biscuits.
William: OK. And a [4]_____ of bananas?
Mum: Yes, please.
William: A [5]_____ of chocolate?
Mum: Yes, I think one will be enough.
William: Olives? Do you mean a [6]_____ of olives?

58 Cambridge Global English Stage 8 Workbook

10: Design and shape

Mum: Yes, and get a big ⁷_____ of crisps.

William: OK. And shall I get two ⁸_____ of water and four ⁹_____ of cola?

Mum: Yes. Oh, and don't forget the yogurt. Get a ¹⁰_____ of strawberry yogurt.

William: A ¹¹_____ of matches? Why do we need matches?

Mum: Well, I've got some nice candles and I thought we could put them in lanterns for when it gets dark.

3 You're going for a picnic with three friends. Write a shopping list of what you need to buy, using the phrases from Exercise 1.

a packet of …

_____   _____
_____   _____
_____   _____
_____   _____

4 Use the expressions in the Language tip box to replace the underlined words in these sentences.

1 Give me <u>two</u> oranges, please.
_____

2 I'll have <u>six</u> eggs, please.
_____

3 There are <u>twenty-four</u> eggs on this tray.
_____

4 Could I have <u>a small number of</u> olives, please?
_____

5 You need <u>twelve</u> eggs for this recipe.
_____

> **Language tip**
>
> **More quantifiers**
> a couple of
> a dozen / half a dozen
> a few
> a number of
>
> *A couple of* means 'two'.
> *Half a dozen* means 'six'.
> *A dozen* means 'twelve'.
> *Two dozen* means 'twenty-four'.
> Notice that you say: *a dozen / half a dozen eggs*
>   NOT
>   *a dozen / half a dozen ~~of~~ eggs*
> You say: *two dozen eggs*
>   NOT
>   *two ~~dozens~~ eggs*
> *A few* means 'a small number of'.

Cambridge Global English Stage 8 Workbook

What shape is it?

1 Label the three-dimensional shapes.

   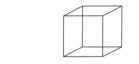

1 s<u>quare</u>-b<u>ased</u> p<u>yramid</u>   2 c _____   3 c _____

4 s _____   5 h _____   6 h _____
                                                                                                                                                                  p _____

7 t _____   8 t _____   9 c _____
   p _____   p _____

2 Fill in the missing words. Use a dictionary to help you.

noun	adjective ending in *-ar*
circle	circular
_____	rectangular
triangle	_____

	adjective ending in *-ical*
_____	spherical
cylinder	_____
mathematics	_____
_____	biological

	adjective ending in *-al*
hexagon	_____
octagon	_____

60 Cambridge Global English Stage 8 Workbook

10: Design and shape

Shape up! A maths quiz

1 How many sides does a triangle have?
   _____

2 A triangle always has sides of equal length. True or false?
   _____

3 What's the difference between a rectangle and a square?
   _____

4 How many sides does a hexagon have?
   _____

   How many sides does an octagon have?
   _____

5 Why is this building called 'The Pentagon'?
   _____

6 If this 'net' was folded into a three-dimensional shape, what would it be?

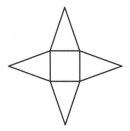

   _____

7 If this 'net' was folded into a three-dimensional shape, what would it be?

   _____

8 If this 'net' was folded into a three-dimensional shape, what would it be?

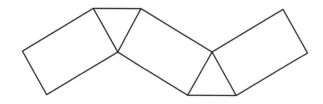

   _____

9 How many cubes are there in this shape?

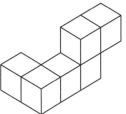

   _____

10 What are these?

   _____

Cambridge Global English Stage 8 Workbook

Classic designs

1 Complete the texts with appropriate words and match them to the photos.

a

b

c

d

1. The original of these were a ¹_____ of sandal worn in ancient Egypt. But ²_____ modern version originated in Japan, where they're ³_____ 'zori'. They're very simple, they're practical and ⁴_____ aren't expensive. You ⁵_____ wear them indoors or outdoors. They ⁶_____ be worn by adults and children. ⁷_____ don't try running in them!
   Photo: _____

2. This item was designed and made ¹_____ Britain in 1932. Since then it ²_____ become popular all over the ³_____ with students, artists, people who work in ⁴_____ and anybody who needs a good light to ⁵_____ what they're doing. It's ⁶_____ practical because you can put it ⁷_____ almost any position.
   Photo: _____

3. It's a classic design that was ¹_____ used for the clocks on railway ²_____ in Switzerland. Its simple design is ³_____ reason for its success.
   Photo: _____

4. This is made of metal and ¹_____ can put candles inside it. Its ²_____, combining straight lines and curves, and ³_____ beautiful, intricate metalwork, make it a ⁴_____ attractive and practical object which would ⁵_____ good in any home.
   Photo: _____

10: Design and shape

2 Find the adjectives to match the definitions. Write them in the spaces.

attractive
classic   modern
comfortable   popular
expensive   practical
intricate   simple
unusual

1 _____: using the most recent styles and ideas in design
2 _____: easy to understand; plain and without decoration
3 _____: useful or suitable for a particular purpose
4 _____: costing a lot of money
5 _____: liked by a lot of people
6 _____: having a style which is always fashionable
7 _____: having many small parts and details
8 _____: pleasant to look at
9 _____: making you feel relaxed, without any pain
10 _____: different and not ordinary

Which adjectives would you use to describe the car in the photo?

_____

3 In your notebook, write a description of this item. Use the texts in Exercise 1 as a model, and try to include the following words:

• simple   • circles   • comfortable   • easy   • rectangular   • attractive

Why is this a design classic?

Cambridge Global English Stage 8 Workbook | 63

11 Personality types

What are you really like?

1 Solve the crossword. All the answers are adjectives describing personality.

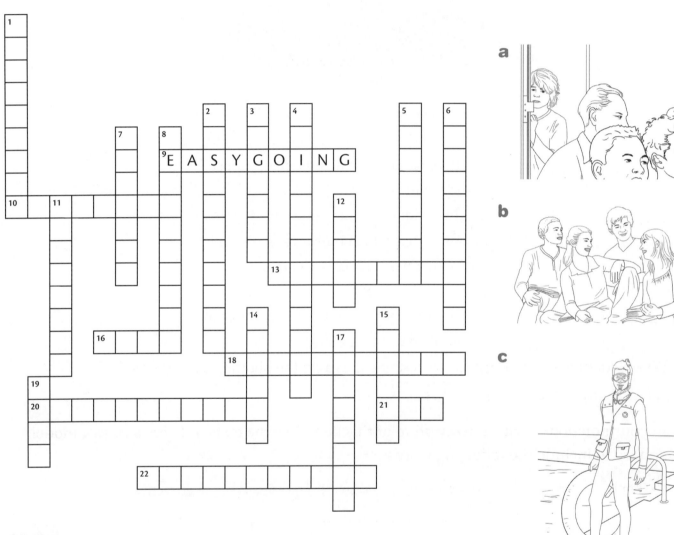

Across
9 I don't easily get upset or worried about things. (4-5)
10 In a difficult situation I know immediately what to do. (8)
13 I hate waiting for people or for things to happen. (9)
16 I like helping other people. (4)
18 I think for myself and I don't need other people to tell me what to do. (11)

11: Personality types

20 I love going to new places and trying new things. (11)
21 I find it a bit frightening to meet new people. (3)
22 I love doing things without planning them. (11)

Down

1 I'm very tidy and I like to plan things carefully. (9)
2 I usually have a negative view of the future. (11)
3 I think in an ordered way and I like solving puzzles. (7)
4 I get angry very easily. (5-8)
5 I love being with people and I've got lots of friends. (8)
6 I always feel positive about the future. (10)
7 I'm the opposite of *13 Across*! (7)
8 Once I've decided to do something, I never give up until I've done it. (10)
11 I don't take risks and I think carefully about things before I do them. (8)
12 Once I've made a friend, they're a friend for life. (5)
14 I always tell the truth. (6)
15 I don't like talking about things I've done well. (6)
17 I'll always give money to people who need it. (8)
19 I'm usually quite relaxed and I don't get nervous about exams. (4)

2 Choose an adjective from the crossword to describe each of the people in the pictures.

a _____   b _____   c _____

3 Complete the sentences with suitable prepositions.

1. Friendship is important _____ me. I have a lot of good friends who are interested _____ the same things as me.

2. I think I'm quite good _____ subjects like English and History. But Maths and Science are quite difficult _____ me.

3. I'd like to be a doctor, but I'm aware _____ how long it takes to train.

4. My mum is very patient. She hardly ever gets annoyed _____ me and she doesn't get upset _____ small things.

A teenage millionaire

1 Complete the sentences about Nick D'Aloisio with the correct prepositions.

1 Nick D'Aloisio's app summarises stories _____ the news.
2 When he was 12, he started designing apps and _____ 15 he launched his own app.
3 _____ home he spends a lot of time working on his computer.
4 He's studying Chinese and Russian _____ school.
5 He wants to study Philosophy _____ university.
6 He doesn't want to work _____ computer programming.

2 Complete the article about Fred Turner with the correct prepositions.

A teenage gene-ious!

¹_____ the age of 17, Fred Turner has been awarded 'UK Young Engineer of the Year'.

Fred has straight brown hair. His brother Gus has curly red hair. Fred was determined to find out why their hair is so different. So he built a DNA testing machine ²_____ his bedroom.

He spent almost a year building the machine, using things he found ³_____ home, including an old video recorder. The machine would normally cost £3000, but Fred built his ⁴_____ £450. It's like a DNA photocopier.

He collected DNA, ⁵_____ inside his brother's cheek. "The machine makes copies of this DNA so you can test how it reacts ⁶_____ different temperatures. Heating and cooling the sample allows you to separate the DNA, so I was able to see whether mine was different ⁷_____ his," said Fred.

He discovered that Gus has a particular gene that gives him red hair.

Fred has always been interested ⁸_____ science and his parents have always encouraged him. "They both took me ⁹_____ science museums when I was younger."

His passion for science will continue ¹⁰_____ Oxford University, where he'll be studying Biochemistry ¹¹_____ September. He said, "I'm not sure where I'll be ¹²_____ ten years, but I'd like to run my own technology business."

3 Answer the questions about the article on page 66.

1 Why did Fred build a DNA testing machine?
_____

2 How is Fred's machine different from a standard testing machine?
_____

3 Why did he need to heat and cool the DNA sample?
_____

4 Why is Gus's hair a different colour from Fred's?
_____

5 What is the link between Fred's early interests and his future plans?
_____

6 Why is the title 'A teenage gene-ious'?
_____

4 Use the fact file to write a paragraph about Ann Makosinski and her invention.

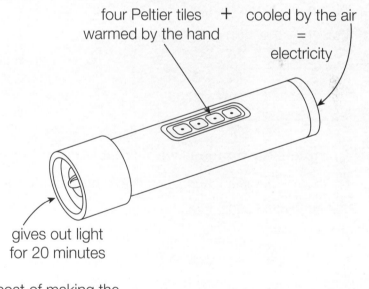

FACT FILE

Name: Ann Makosinski
Age: 15
Award: first prize at a global science fair in California
Reason for invention: to help a friend in the Philippines who couldn't do her homework after dark
Invention: torch powered by heat from the hand

four Peltier tiles warmed by the hand + cooled by the air = electricity

gives out light for 20 minutes

cost of making the torch: 26 dollars

At the age of …
_____
_____

The world of soap opera

1 Match the words with the definitions.

1 bravery
2 jealousy
3 greed
4 ambition
5 anger
6 loyalty
7 arrogance
8 modesty

a determination to be rich, powerful or successful
b when you want a lot more money, power or possessions than you need
c a strong feeling of unhappiness because someone you like or love is interested in someone else, or because you haven't got something and someone else has it
d the feeling of strong friendship, which means that you will do anything to help a friend or someone you love
e when you are able to deal with a dangerous situation without fear
f when you do not talk proudly about what you have achieved
g when you think you are better and more important than other people
h a strong negative emotion that comes from feeling that you have been badly treated

2 Write the adjectives for each of the nouns in Exercise 1.

	Noun	Adjective			
1	bravery	He's/She's _brave_.	5	_____	_____
2	_____	_____	6	_____	_____
3	_____	_____	7	_____	_____
4	_____	_____	8	_____	_____

3 Complete the opinions with suitable nouns or adjectives from Exercise 2.

"Soap operas are about very clear human emotions; for example, [1]____*jealousy*____. A man becomes [2]_____ because his wife is very beautiful and it takes over his whole personality."

"People in soap operas are often determined to succeed and get to the top – they're very [3]_____. And they want more and more money – they're [4]_____. Yes, [5]_____ and [6]_____ are very powerful emotions in soap operas."

"There are also strong positive emotions: love, for example. Characters are always falling in and out of love. Then there's the wife who is always [7]_____ to her husband, even though she knows he's done something wrong. Her [8]_____ to him can put her in danger, or even make her commit a crime."

"People can often do things which show they are not afraid, even in quite dangerous situations. [9]_____ is an important emotion in soap opera."

Cambridge Global English Stage 8 Workbook

11: Personality types

4 Create your own soap opera!

You are going to write a profile of a character from a soap opera.

In your next class, you are going to introduce yourself to other members of the class as if you were this person.

Name: _____
Why have you chosen this name? What does it say about the person?
_____

Age: _____
Family:
Are you single or married? Are you happy?
_____

Personality: _____
How do other people see you?
_____

Ambition: _____
Is your ambition realistic?
_____

Strong point of your character: _____
Weak point of your character: _____
What has just happened to you before the opening of the first episode of your soap opera?

_____
_____
_____
_____
_____
_____

5 In your next class, work in small groups. Ask questions to find out about the characters other members of the group have invented.

6 In your groups, imagine the storyline of the first episode of your new soap opera.

Cambridge Global English Stage 8 Workbook

12 People and their jobs

The world of work

1 What are the jobs?

1
musician

2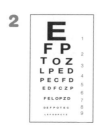
_____

3
_____

4
_____

5
_____

6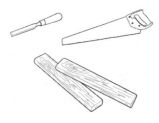
_____

2 Complete the sentences.

1 I've got a problem with my teeth. Do you know a good __dentist__?
2 I want to study Medicine because I want to be a _____.
3 I'd like to learn to drive. Can you recommend a good _____?
4 Mum and Dad both work. They haven't got time to clean the house, so they employ a _____.
5 Oh no! There's water all over the kitchen floor. I think the water pipe has burst. Call the _____.
6 Our neighbour knows a lot about cars. He's a _____ at the local garage.
7 This light switch has broken. Do you know an _____ we can call?
8 My aunt studied Engineering at university. She now works on big building projects all over the world. She's an _____.

12: People and their jobs

3 In your notebook, describe the jobs these people do. If you can, say where they work.

1 A physiotherapist <u>uses special exercises, heat or massage to help people recover from an injury. A physiotherapist works in a hospital.</u>
2 A receptionist
3 A taxi driver
4 A waiter/waitress
5 A shop assistant
6 A paramedic
7 A farm worker
8 A journalist
9 A hairdresser
10 A flight attendant

4 Complete the text with appropriate words.

1 The taxi driver

You have to like people, doing [1]_____ job I do. And you have [2]_____ be very patient because sometimes the [3]_____ is quite heavy and it takes [4]_____ long time to get from A [5]_____ B but you do meet some [6]_____ people.

2 The paramedic

In my job, one of the [1]_____ important things is to stay calm [2]_____ sometimes it's a matter of life [3]_____ death. We give emergency first aid [4]_____, if necessary, we have to get [5]_____ to hospital as quickly as possible. [6]_____ is important to be decisive, to [7]_____ able to make the right decision [8]_____ the right time.

3 The engineer

My job is both an indoor [1]_____ an outdoor job. I spend quite [2]_____ lot of time in the office [3]_____ on plans for buildings and bridges, [4]_____ so on. But I also spend [5]_____ lot of time on site, working [6]_____ architects and builders. My job really [7]_____ me because it's about practical things.

4 The waiter

My job's quite tiring. I'm on [1]_____ feet all day. You have to [2]_____ patient too. Most customers are really [3]_____, but there are one or two [4]_____ are just so difficult to please. [5]_____ say, "This isn't what I ordered," [6]_____ you know it was what they [7]_____. Or "This is too salty" or "[8]_____ is too spicy". But you have [9]_____ remember, the customer is always right.

5 The physiotherapist

I work at the health centre, [1]_____ I also do some work at [2]_____ local football club because I specialised [3]_____ sports injuries when I did my [4]_____. It's important to get people moving [5]_____ after an injury or an operation, [6]_____ you have to do it very [7]_____.

A day in the life

1 Read what people say about their jobs and complete the words.

1 I'm part of a mountain rescue team. When someone's lost or in trouble on the mountain, we get a call and we go out and look for them. We don't get paid. We're all vo_____ .

2 I work in a wildlife park as a park warden. My regular du_____ include feeding the animals, checking that they've got water, checking the fences, and that sort of thing.

3 I'm training to work in a call centre for receiving calls for the fire service, the police or the ambulance. You have to learn to be calm so that you can deal with em_____ , such as traffic accidents, fires or crimes.

4 I'm a dentist. I studied for five years at university and then I worked at a health centre for a few years. Now I'm setting up my own practice, so I need to buy a lot of expensive eq_____ .

5 I'm a farmer. We only have a few people working on the farm now because most of the work can be done with ma_____ .

6 I'm a firefighter. As part of my job, I go out to check buildings to make sure everything is OK. These building in_____ are very important because they show whether buildings are safe.

7 I work in IT as a computer programmer. You have to make sure you keep up with new te_____ .

8 I work as a nurse. Sometimes I work during the day and sometimes I do the night sh_____ .

2 Which of the jobs in Exercise 1 would you do? Which of the jobs wouldn't you do?

I wouldn't mind being a _____
because _____
_____.

I wouldn't enjoy being a _____
because _____
_____.

Cambridge Global English Stage 8 Workbook

12: People and their jobs

3 Complete the text with the correct *-ing* forms of the verbs in the box.

• be • call • check • do • get up • give • give up • watch • work

I work as a doctor in the Accident & Emergency department of a big hospital. I'm also a volunteer at motor racing events. I don't mind ¹_____ my free time because I enjoy ²_____ the races. Also, as a hospital doctor, I spend all of my time ³_____ inside, so at the end of a hard week it's good to do something that involves ⁴_____ outside. My duties at race meetings include ⁵_____ drivers who have had accidents, as well as ⁶_____ first aid before ⁷_____ the emergency services when necessary. Sometimes I don't feel like ⁸_____ early on a Saturday morning to drive a long way to an event. However, I always enjoy it when I get there, so I keep on ⁹_____ it!

4 Rewrite these sentences.

1 A good chef makes a new dish several times before serving it to customers.
(Use *practise*)
A good chef <u>practises making a new dish before serving it to customers.</u>

2 If you're a firefighter, you have to take risks.
(Use *can't avoid*)
If you're a firefighter, you _____

3 My great-grandfather is 92 and he has only just stopped driving.
(Use *give up*)
My great-grandfather is 92 and he _____

4 Being a good doctor means that you have to listen to people.
(Use *involve*)
Being a good doctor _____

5 You can't be a good department store manager if you don't enjoy team work.
(Use *without*)
You can't be a good department store manager _____

6 If you want to work in marketing, it's a good idea to do a business course.
(Use *should think about*)
If you want to work in marketing, _____

Cambridge Global English Stage 8 Workbook

What about becoming a ... ?

1 Read the survey information about jobs.

> **What will you be doing in ten years' time?**
> Top 20 most popular choices for jobs for 13- to 14-year-olds
>
> | | | |
> |---|---|---|
> | 1 Actor / Actress | 8 Accountant | 15 Vet |
> | 2 Lawyer | 9 Armed forces / Firefighter | 16 TV / Radio presenter or DJ |
> | 3 Police officer | 10 Singer / Musician | 17 Artist |
> | 4 Doctor | 11 IT consultant | 18 Manager (e.g. in an office, factory) |
> | 5 Sportsman / woman | 12 Graphic designer | 19 Hairdresser |
> | 6 Teacher / Lecturer | 13 Designer (e.g. fashion) | 20 Beauty therapist |
> | 7 Chef | 14 Dancer | |

Which jobs do you associate with these places? (There may be more than one job for some of the places.)

- **a** animal clinic — vet
- **b** concert hall _____
- **c** fire station _____
- **d** hospital _____
- **e** law courts _____
- **f** office _____
- **g** restaurant _____
- **h** salon _____
- **i** school or college _____
- **j** stadium _____
- **k** studio _____
- **l** theatre _____

2 Which jobs from the survey are these people talking about? Complete what they're saying with the correct word.

1 It's a good job because you can earn a lot of money, but I'm also interested in helping people when they're in trouble. By the time I'm 20, I hope I'll be studying Law at university. It'll be a lot of work, but it'll be worth it in the end. By the time I'm 30, I hope I'll be a successful _____.

2 It's a fantastic job, but you don't always have work. My plan is to go to drama school when I'm 18 and then I'll go to as many auditions as possible. I don't mind having small parts in plays or films to begin with. That's the way you learn. By the time I'm 25, I think I'll be a successful _____. I'll be living in Hollywood and I'll be starring in major feature films.

12: People and their jobs

3 I'm really interested in clothes and I enjoy creating new styles. I want to do a university course that's practical. I'd love to do work experience in Milan with one of the top names. I don't mind doing basic jobs to start with, if it helps me to learn about the industry. I hope that by the time I'm 30, I'll be a top _____ myself and that I'll be selling the clothes I make from my own shop.

3 In your notebook, write a paragraph, similar to the ones in Exercise 2, about your ambitions. Include some or all of the following phrases:

I'm interested in …   By the time I'm (25), …   I'd like to / I'd love to …
I enjoy …   I don't mind …   I hope that …

4 Read the information in the leaflet about becoming a vet. Then answer the questions.

So you want to be a vet?

You need to care about animals. You need to be strong and decisive. You need to be good at solving problems. It's also important to have good communication skills, so that you can talk to the animals' owners. And you need to be able to write good letters and emails.

It takes five years to study to be a vet. To study Veterinary Medicine at university, you will need qualifications in Biology, Chemistry and another subject, such as Maths.

It's a good idea to get work experience on farms, in veterinary clinics, at riding stables or in animal homes. This will show that you're really keen on becoming a vet and it will help you get a place on a university course.

Being a vet means working long hours, doing a lot of office work and being on call at night for emergencies. However, it's quite a well-paid job and you are helping to improve the health and happiness of animals.

1 What sort of person do you need to be? _____
2 What skills do you need? _____
3 Do you need a university degree to do this job? _____
4 What qualifications do you need to be accepted on a university course?
   _____
5 What else is useful if you want to get on to a university course?
   _____
6 How long is the training? _____
7 Is the job well paid? _____
8 What's good about the job? _____
9 Are there any disadvantages? _____

13 Shops and services

In the aisles

1 Write the names of the supermarket sections on the signs.

- bakery
- dairy products
- frozen foods
- health and beauty
- home baking
- household and cleaning
- stationery
- tinned foods

1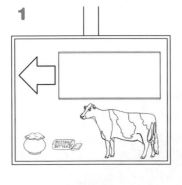

2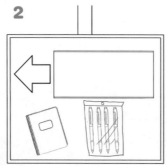

3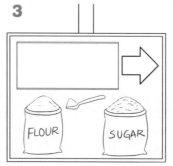

4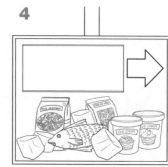

5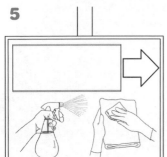

6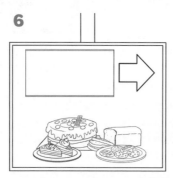

7

8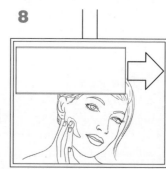

2 In which section of the supermarket would you find the following? Write the number of the section from Exercise 1 beside each item.

a bag of sugar	3	a carton of ice cream	
a bar of soap		a carton of milk	
a bottle of shampoo		four tins of tomatoes	
a bottle of washing-up liquid		250g of butter	
six bread rolls		a notebook	

Cambridge Global English Stage 8 Workbook

3 Complete the supermarket announcements with the correct prepositions.

1 Today, in the bakery section, we have a special offer of three loaves of bread _____ the price _____ two.
2 This week, there's 20% _____ selected brands of shampoo, so stock up now!
3 We have delicious cream cakes _____ offer this week at half price. Don't miss them!
4 Camping equipment and garden furniture are _____ sale at our store this month. So get ready for summer!
5 All fresh fruit is down _____ 10% this week. That's great for a healthy diet!
6 A special deal _____ fresh noodles: buy one packet and get one free!

Learning words in groups

It can be helpful to learn words in categories, using a word web.
Add items to these supermarket categories.

- dairy products
  - cheese
- bakery
- health and beauty
- household and cleaning

Study skills

4 Which offers in Exercise 3 do these signs refer to?

A 50% discount

B Buy two and get the third free

C Four for ~~£1~~ 90p

D Get two for the price of one

The psychology of shopping

1 Complete the words. (They're all connected with shopping.)

1 It's a good idea to write this before you start: s _ _ _ _ _ _ _ g l _ _ t
2 Next find one of these: t _ _ _ _ _ y
3 Or this: b _ _ _ _ t
4 Then off you go. To find everything you need, you probably have to go down all the a _ _ _ _ _ s
5 But if you just pop into the supermarket because you're hungry and in a hurry, you can buy one of these: s _ _ _ _ _ _ h
6 You can probably find number 5 near the e _ _ _ _ _ _ e
7 But don't forget to pay at the c _ _ _ _ _ _ t

2 Match the two halves of each sentence.

1 The freshly baked bread smells so good
2 You can select and weigh
3 The most tempting food is at eye level,
4 You can find everything you need in one place,
5 You often spend
6 The signs above the aisles
7 Supermarkets are designed
8 Supermarkets provide large trolleys,

a make it easy to find what you're looking for.
b more than you had planned.
c so it saves you time.
d that you buy two loaves, even though there's only one on your list.
e so you sometimes buy things you hadn't thought you needed.
f the fruit and vegetables yourself.
g so it's easy to carry all your shopping.
h to make sure you go down every aisle.

3 Which four sentences in Exercise 2 describe the definite advantages of shopping at a supermarket?

_____ _____
_____ _____

4 Complete the table by writing in the reflexive pronouns.

Subject pronouns	Reflexive pronouns
I	myself
you (singular)	
he	
she	
it	
we	
you (plural)	
they	

13: Shops and services

5 Complete the sentences with the correct reflexive pronouns.
1 Try some of this bread. I made it _____ .
2 Now, all of you, remember: don't panic. Give _____ time to read the questions.
3 'Do I really need this?' We should all ask _____ this question when we're out shopping!
4 Tom, help _____ to another slice of cake.
5 You can set the timer on the oven, so that it switches _____ off when the food is cooked.
6 My grandparents have just bought _____ a new electric car.
7 She had a terrible shock when she saw _____ in the mirror after she'd coloured her hair.

6 Answer these questions about a recent shopping trip to a supermarket.
1 Did you do the shopping yourself or did you go with someone?
_____
2 Did you have a trolley or a basket?
_____
3 Did you go down all the aisles?
_____
4 Which sections did you go to? What did you buy there?
_____
5 What did you find most tempting?
_____
6 Did you buy just the essentials, or were you tempted to buy more?
_____
7 Did you buy anything that was on offer?
_____

7 In your notebook, write a paragraph about a recent trip to a supermarket. Use your answers to Exercise 6 to help you. Try to add an amusing detail if you can.

A trip to the supermarket
_____
_____
_____

Cambridge Global English Stage 8 Workbook

The best present

1 Complete the sentences in column A with the words and phrases in columns B and C.

A	B	C
1 How much did you	belonged	to my great-grandmother.
2 She's really kind. She always	depends	of being a racing driver.
3 This necklace	don't agree	of other people before herself.
4 I like him, but I	looking	on the weather.
5 It would be nice to go for a picnic, but it	dreamed	with everything he says.
6 When he was young, he	pay	for that jacket? It's really nice.
7 Sorry, I can't	wait	for his sunglasses, but they were on his head.
8 He spent ten minutes	thinks	for you any longer.

1 _____
2 _____
3 _____
4 _____
5 _____
6 _____
7 _____
8 _____

2 Complete the sentences with the correct prepositions.

1 I don't understand the maths homework. Can you explain it _____ me?
2 If you get lost, you can ask _____ directions.
3 What time does the train arrive _____ Paris?
4 It arrives _____ midnight.
5 You're really late. What happened _____ you?
6 He's really boring. He's always talking _____ himself.
7 The teacher couldn't help smiling _____ Hugo's silly joke.
8 Will you look _____ my cat while I'm away on holiday?

13: Shops and services

3 Write a suitable caption for each picture using an adjective followed by a preposition.

1
He was very *good at long jump*.

2
She's always been _____.

3
She always been _____.

4
He's always been _____.

5
He was very _____.

6
She was really _____.

4 Think of an everyday object. In your notebook, write clues to describe it without naming it. In the next lesson, show the clues to your classmate to see if he or she can guess what the object is.

They're not expensive.
They can be any colour.
They're useful when it's hot and especially when you're at the beach.
You can buy them at a supermarket or a sports shop.
You wear them on your feet.

Cambridge Global English Stage 8 Workbook

14 Possessions and personal space

Treasured possessions

1 Read what the people in column A say. What did they go on to say? Find the answers in column B.

A

1. My most treasured possession is my signed copy of *War Horse* by Michael Morpurgo.
2. My most prized possession is my One Direction poster.
3. One of my favourite things is a jigsaw puzzle which my grandma gave me.
4. I really treasure my ticket for the concert to raise money for people who lost their homes in the tsunami last year.
5. All my sports and dance trophies are special to me.
6. I would say my photo of my whole family is my most treasured possession.
7. My most prized possession is my silver necklace.
8. I love my cats.
9. My most treasured possession is my old teddy bear.
10. I love my bed. I wouldn't be able to live without it.

B

a. They run out to meet me when I come home from school. *Lily*
b. I wear it all the time and I have had it since I was born. I love my jewellery box too. *Jade*
c. I've had him since I was a baby. He's called Ted. He's scruffy, but I love him to bits. *Katya*
d. It was given to her by her grandma, so it's really old. *Amber*
e. It was signed by all the members of the band. *Abbie*
f. It's somewhere I can be lazy and do nothing at all. *Karem*
g. Some of the people in it aren't around any more – that's why it's important to me. *Oliver*
h. That was the best day of my life and I knew I was doing something for people who needed help. *George*
i. I've read it over and over again. *Alice*
j. When I look at them I remember how hard I worked to win them. *Maya*

1 ___	2 ___	3 ___	4 ___	5 ___
6 ___	7 ___	8 ___	9 ___	10 ___

14: Possessions and personal space

2 Read about these treasured possessions. Why do you think each person chose that particular thing? Imagine you are that person and give your reason for choosing it.

1 "My most treasured possession is my diary.
_____"

2 "I treasure a photo of me and all my classmates at primary school.
_____"

3 "My hockey trophies are my most prized possessions.
_____"

4 " One of my favourite possessions is my mum's really old bedtime story book.
_____"

5 "I treasure my notebook. I take it with me everywhere.
_____"

6 "I couldn't live without my mobile!
_____"

3 Look at the signs. What can you have done at these places?

1   You can have your hair cut.

2   _____

3   _____

4   _____

5   _____

6   _____

My space

1 Complete the conversation with suitable words.

Interviewer: You've got a great room here. ¹_____ us a guided tour.

Yann: Well, where ²_____ I start? I've got bunk beds ³_____ I share my room with my ⁴_____.

Interviewer: And there's a ladder to get ⁵_____ the top bed.

Yann: Mine's the bottom ⁶_____.

Interviewer: Is that your snowboard? It looks ⁷_____. How long have you had it?

Yann: ⁸_____ have only had it for a ⁹_____ months. I saved up for it ¹⁰_____ quite a long time.

2 Report the underlined sentences using the past perfect and making any other necessary changes.

Zara: Wow! Your room looks really good.

Jamila: Yes, ¹my mum's just had the bedrooms repainted.

Zara: It's really nice. It's very colourful.

Jamila: Thanks. ²I chose the colours myself.

Zara: You're very tidy.

Jamila: ³I've just put everything away in the cupboard.

Zara: I really like these little boxes.

Jamila: ⁴I've had the jewellery box for ages. It belonged to my grandmother.

Zara: Who are these people in the photo?

Jamila: Oh, that's my uncle and aunt and cousins. ⁵My uncle and aunt have just gone to live in Sweden.

Zara: You've got lots of books on your bookshelf. What are you reading at the moment?

Jamila: ⁶I've just finished reading *The Village by the Sea*. I don't know what I'm going to read next.

1 *She said her mum had just had the bedrooms repainted.*

2 _____

3 _____

4 _____

5 _____

6 _____

3 Look at the pictures and spot eight differences. Write them in your notebook.

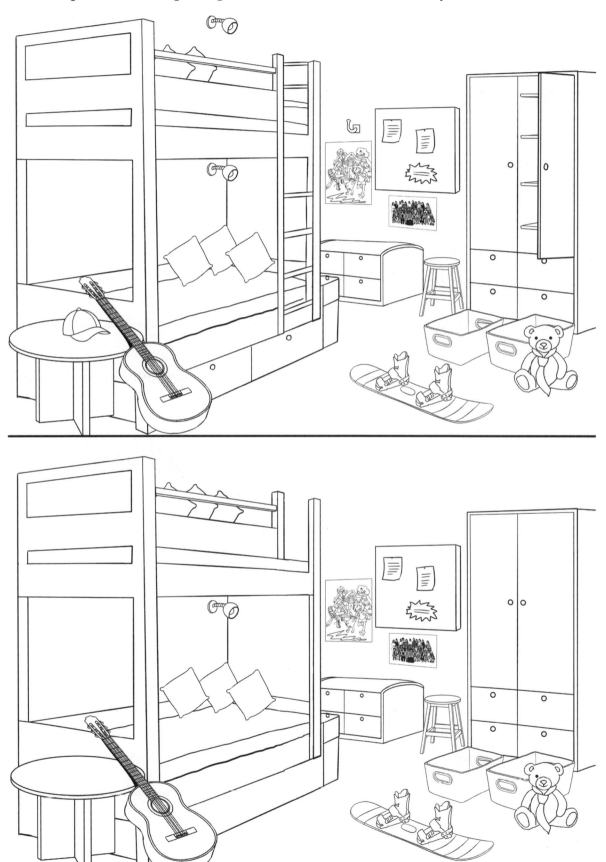

For sale

1 Complete the sentences with compound adjectives.

1. These eggs are fresh from the farm.
They are _farm-fresh_ eggs.

2. I made this cake at home.
It's a _____-_____ cake.

3. My friend's house has got four storeys.
It's a _____-_____ house.

4. She's good at running long distances.
She's a _____-_____ runner.

5. These tomatoes were dried in the sun.
They're _____-_____ tomatoes.

6. This water is as cold as ice.
It's _____-_____ water.

7. He's a photographer and he's famous all over the world.
He's a _____-_____ photographer.

8. She likes to go for a swim early in the morning.
She enjoys an _____-_____ swim.

2 What do the compound adjectives on these labels mean? Complete the explanations.

1. This drink has _____.

2. This energy bar doesn't _____.

 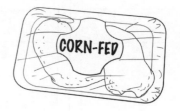

3. There is _____ in this yogurt.

4. This chicken has _____.

5. These crisps haven't _____.

Cambridge Global English Stage 8 Workbook

14: Possessions and personal space

Study skills

Using compound adjectives

Compound adjectives are more common in writing than in conversation. You can use them as an economical and effective way of describing something. For example, look back at the compound adjectives you wrote in Exercise 1.

3 Make compound adjectives by taking one word from each column. Then think of a noun that each one could describe and use it in a sentence.

English	blue
good	looking
pale	loving
high	selling
best	speaking
fun	speed

1 _Canada is an English-speaking country._
2 _____
3 _____
4 _____
5 _____
6 _____

4 Complete the restaurant review with the compound adjectives in the box.

- brightly-lit
- carefully-planned
- freshly-baked
- honey-coloured
- recently-restored
- snow-white
- world-famous

The Dining Room is a ¹ _recently-restored_ restaurant in a Scottish castle. The heavy old doors lead you to expect a dark, gloomy interior. However, they open to reveal a ² _____ entrance hall, which is immediately welcoming. Then, as soon as you walk into the restaurant, you smell the ³ _____ bread which will soon appear on your table. The ⁴ _____ natural stone walls contrast beautifully with the dazzling ⁵ _____ tablecloths. The only problem you will have is knowing what to choose from the ⁶ _____ menu, created by the ⁷ _____ chef, Alain Robert.

15 Natural disasters

Dangerous nature

1 Read the clues and write the words in the grid to reveal the mystery word.

Clues
1 The force pressing on something.
2 A strong wall built across a river to stop the water from flowing.
3 Where a river starts or where something comes from.
4 You can eat off these, but they are also large pieces of rock which form the surface of the earth.
5 A violent storm with very strong winds.
6 It goes around the middle of the earth.
7 The outside of a loaf of bread and the outer layer of the earth.
8 Fast and continuous shaking movements.
9 The sides of a river.
10 With fuel and a heat source, it makes up the fire triangle.

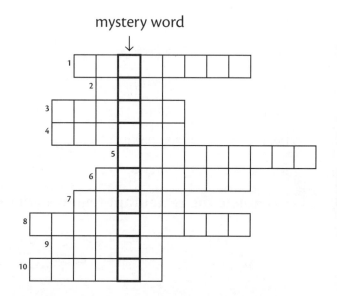

2 Complete the text with the prepositions from the box.

• against   • at (x2)   • in (x2)   • near   • over   • up

Wildfires can move ¹_____ speeds of over 20 kilometres an hour. They burn everything ²_____ their path.

In an earthquake, the earth's plates press ³_____ each other, causing pressure to build up. Vibrations travel ⁴_____ to the earth's surface. The energy is released ⁵_____ waves, which are strongest ⁶_____ the epicentre.

Hurricanes start ⁷_____ the water ⁸_____ the equator.

3 Read the news website report. Complete it using the present perfect passive of the verbs in brackets.

Have you been affected by the flooding?

Some villages and small towns [1](cut off) _have been cut off_ by the flood water. This [2](cause) _____ by heavy rain and by rivers bursting their banks. Many parts of the country have had their wettest January since records began, more than a hundred years ago. The village of Muchelney in the south west of England [3](turn into) _____ an island. Two hundred villagers [4](trap) _____ for the last ten days because the village [5](cut off) _____ completely for over a week. The village can only be reached by boat or canoe. A rescue boat from the coast [6](bring) _____ to the village to bring in supplies. It [7](also/use) _____ to take children to and from school. Some animals, such as cows and sheep, [8](move) _____ because their fields were flooded.

Have you missed school?
[9](your school/close) _____ because of the weather? Email us and let us know.
"We [10](cut off) _____ by the flood water for nearly two weeks now. We can't go by car, but we [11](take) _____ to and from school every day in the rescue boat."
"We can't go outside and play, or ride our bikes, because our house is surrounded by flood water. Luckily our house [12](not flood) _____."

Drought in East Africa

A

Water For All

Nearly 800 million people in the world do not have access to clean water. That's about one in ten of the world's population.

Our mission is to overcome poverty by giving the world's poorest people access to clean water and sanitation.

Clean water improves hygiene and saves lives. Simply being able to wash your hands prevents disease.

With a donation of just £15, you can give someone a safe supply of clean water for life.

B

Child Action

Give children a chance. With your help, we can provide shelter, food, water and education to a child who has lost everything.

Sponsor a child now.

Your generosity can save lives and help millions of children.

C

Make hunger history

Hungry?

Can you imagine what it's like to be hungry every day? Could you survive on a fraction of what you eat every day? Think about it. Give what you can to make hunger history.

15: Natural disasters

1 Find the words and phrases on the posters for the following.
1. An aim that is very important to a person or an organisation.
2. To succeed in controlling a problem, to fight and win against something or someone.
3. A system for protecting people's health by removing dirt and waste.
4. Keeping yourself and your surroundings clean in order to prevent disease.
5. A gift of money to help a person or organisation.
6. A place to live.
7. Agree to give money to help someone who lives in another country.
8. A very small number or amount.

2 Read the comments and choose those which you think best describe each poster/leaflet.

It gives a positive message about what the charity is trying to do. _____

It makes you realise that some people don't have even the most basic things. _____

It makes you think about how much you have and how little others have. _____

It tells you what the money is used for. _____

It works because it tells you how a small amount of money could make a big difference. _____

It's effective because it makes you compare your life with other people's situations. _____

It works because it gives a clear and simple message. _____

It gives you information about a particular problem. _____

3 Rewrite the sentences using the structures in brackets. Complete them in an appropriate way.
1. Although she had very little money, she always …
   (use *despite*)
   Despite having very little money, she always gave donations to charity.
2. Although there were serious floods, the rescue services managed to …
   (use *in spite of*)

3. Although we collected a lot of money for famine relief, we still …
   (use *despite*)

4. Although it's not a drought area, a lot of people don't have …
   (use *in spite of*)

Cambridge Global English Stage 8 Workbook   91

Raising money for charity

1 Solve the crossword.

Across

3 An animal that looks like a small horse with long ears. (6)
6 A glass container. (3)
8 A person who takes part in a competition. (10)
9 You get this for winning or for doing something well. (5)
11 Stay on the surface of a liquid. (5)
12 To hit something, or someone, and make it, or them, move or fall down. (5)
13 In the game of apple bobbing, you have to pick up the apple with your _____. (5)

Down

1 It's smaller than a town. (7)
2 It grows on a tree, it's dark brown with a hard hairy shell and inside it's white. (7)
4 Money or gifts given to help people who are poor or sick. (7)
5 An open container with a handle used for carrying water. (6)
7 With your eyes covered. (11)
9 It's a charity fête game called '_____ the tail on the 3 Across'. (3)
10 A large bag made of cloth or paper. (4)

92 Cambridge Global English Stage 8 Workbook

2 Complete the rules for the games. Use the following phrases:

• You have to • You can • You can't • You must • You mustn't

1
Obstacle course

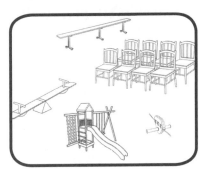

£1 per circuit
prize if you get round without touching the ground
You pay £1 to do the obstacle course.
You have to …
_____

2
Beat the goalie

each contestant three kicks
stand on or behind the line
a prize for each goal
_____
_____
_____

3
Egg and spoon race

one hand only
hold the egg? No.
pick up the egg with your hand if you drop it? No.
_____
_____
_____

4
Hoopla

three hoops for each contestant
a hoop completely over prize wins it
(not resting on or half over the prize)
_____
_____
_____

16 Survivors

Amazing survival

1 Use a suitable word to complete the definitions of the underlined words and phrases.

1 Juliane Köepcke was flying to Lima in Peru when lightning struck the plane and there was an <u>explosion</u>.

A sudden loud __bang/noise/sound__ often caused by something like a bomb.

2 She lost <u>consciousness</u>.

The state of being awake and able to hear, _____ and think.

3 When she <u>came round</u>, she had fallen 3000 metres through the air into the Peruvian rainforest.

Became _____ again after being unconscious.

4 She was still <u>strapped</u> into her seat.

Held in position by a _____ belt.

5 She had cuts and <u>bruises</u>.

Purple or brown marks on the _____ as a result of falling or being hit.

6 She had also broken her <u>collarbone</u>.

One of the two bones that go from the bottom of your neck to your _____.

7 She was the only <u>survivor</u> out of the 92 people on board.

Somebody who is still alive after an event that could have _____ them.

8 Her <u>survival instinct</u> took over and she walked for ten days in the rainforest before she was found.

A strong _____ that you want to carry on living.

9 "I have learned that life is <u>precious</u>," she says.

Something that is _____ and that shouldn't be wasted.

10 '<u>Trivial</u> things don't worry me any more.'

Small and not _____.

2 Complete the text with suitable words.

Bahia Bakari was 12 years old ¹_____ the time. She was going to ²_____ Comoros Islands near Madagascar, off the east ³_____ of Africa, when the plane in ⁴_____ she was travelling crashed into the ⁵_____ Ocean. There were 153 passengers on ⁶_____ and she was the only survivor. ⁷_____ escaped with a broken collarbone and ⁸_____ . She was in the sea for 13 ⁹_____ before she was rescued.

16: Survivors

3 Read the text in Exercise 2 again and write questions for these answers.

1 Q <u>How old was Bahia Bakari when the accident happened?</u>

A She was 12 years old.

2 Q _____

A To the Comoros Islands.

3 Q _____

A Off the coast of east Africa, near Madagascar.

4 Q _____

A The plane crashed into the Indian Ocean.

5 Q _____

A 153.

6 Q _____

A Only one.

7 Q _____

A Yes, she broke her collarbone and she had burns.

8 Q _____

A 13 hours.

4 Look at the words in the Study skills box. Try to visualise them. Then cover the list and write the words out.

5 The letters for the [ʃ] sound in these words are missing. Write them in.

1 cra ____
2 ____ ocked
3 pa ____ ent
4 spe ____ al
5 musi ____ an
6 ____ elf
7 deli ____ ous
8 na ____ onal
9 ____ irt
10 ma ____ ine

> **Study skills**
>
> **Spelling and pronunciation: Visualising words**
>
> In English, the same sound can be spelt in different ways. Look at these words, for example, which all contain the [ʃ] sound, as in *she*:
>
> <u>sh</u>e
>
> destina<u>ti</u>on
>
> con<u>sci</u>ousness
>
> pre<u>ci</u>ous
>
> pre<u>ss</u>ure
>
> o<u>ce</u>an

Cambridge Global English Stage 8 Workbook

Surviving together

1 These words and phrases all appear in the article about the Chilean miners on page 126 of the Coursebook. Match them to their meanings.

1 collapsed
2 trapped
3 ventilation
4 to keep their spirits up
5 drilling
6 signs of life
7 broke through
8 capsule
9 shafts
10 steel
11 navy
12 estimated

a a container with straight sides and rounded ends.
b a military force that operates at sea
c evidence that a person is alive
d fell down
e guessed by using knowledge and experience
f long narrow passages that lead from the surface of the ground into a mine
g making a hole using a special machine
h movement of air around a room or building
i strong metal made from iron and carbon
j to help them remain cheerful
k unable to escape
l went through using force

2 Choose words from the box to complete the compound nouns.

| • copper | • hole | • emergency | • majority |
| • broadcasts | • operation | • ventilation | • video |

1 news _____
2 _____ camera
3 drill _____
4 _____ mine
5 rescue _____
6 _____ supplies
7 _____ system
8 _____ vote

3 Complete these collocations with the correct prepositions.
1 The rescuers drilled carefully to see if they could find any signs _____ life.
2 The miners were brought up one _____ one in the capsule.
3 People _____ the world watched the news broadcasts on TV.

16: Survivors

4 Match the two parts of the verb phrases. Then use each one in a sentence which shows its meaning.

keep	as a team
take	your spirits up
work	decisions

1 _____
2 _____
3 _____

5 Complete the sentences using comparative adverbs made from the following adjectives.

• careful   • cheap   • easy   • quiet   • slow

1 You can buy fruit and vegetables __more cheaply__ at the market.
2 We would have found the place _____ if we had looked at the map before we set out.
3 You will need to check your work _____ if you want to get a good mark.
4 I know you like driving quickly, but if you drive _____ we can enjoy the view.
5 If you practise the piano after 9.30 in the evening, you will have to play _____.

6 The following adverbs have -er endings in the comparative. Use them with *much* to complete the sentences below.

Adverb	Comparative form
early	earlier
fast	faster
hard	harder
late	later
soon	sooner

1 They were very early. They arrived __much earlier__ than I expected.
2 We finished work _____ today because we had a lot to do.
3 I worked _____ for this exam than I did for the last one.
4 My grandmother drives like a bank robber. She drives _____ than my mum.
5 Spring has arrived _____ than usual this year.

Cambridge Global English Stage 8 Workbook

Survival kit

1 Solve the crossword.

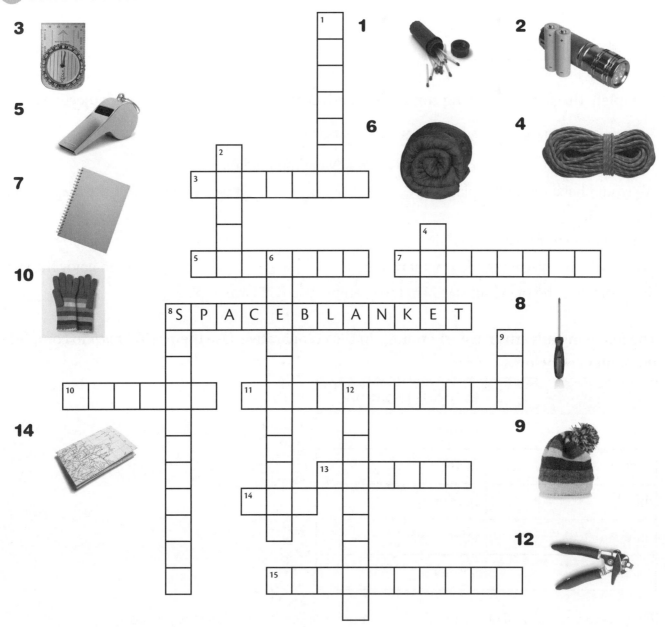

Across

3 See picture 3. (7)
5 See picture 5. (7)
7 See picture 7. (8)
8 You need this to keep you warm in an emergency (5, 7)
10 See picture 10. (6)
11 It contains plasters, antiseptic wipes and bandages (5-3, 3)
13 A container for water (6)
14 See picture 14. (3)
15 Your jacket must be _____, so that you don't get wet in the rain (10)

16: Survivors

Down
1 See picture 1. (7)
2 See picture 2. (5)
4 See picture 4. (4)
6 See picture 6. (8, 3)
8 See picture 8. (11)
9 See picture 9. (3)
12 See picture 12. (3, 6)

2 Write each question above the paragraph to which it refers.

Have I got the clothes I need for this expedition?
What can I borrow?
What's the weather going to be like?
How long am I going for?
What should my first-aid kit have in it?

Ask yourself these questions.

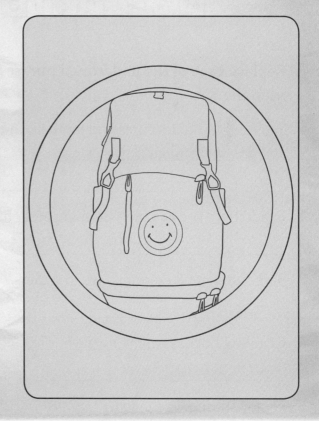

1 _____
A two-day trip is very different from a three- or four-day expedition. Make sure you have what you need for the number of days. Think of food rations.

2 _____
Check what's already in your wardrobe. Avoid items made of denim and cotton.

3 _____
Ask around. See if anybody will lend you small items like a hat, a torch, a multi-tool or a space blanket.

4 _____
Make sure you have plasters, bandages and antiseptic wipes.

5 _____
You must have a waterproof jacket and preferably trousers too. Do you need suncream, a sun hat or sun glasses? Check the forecast. Remember that conditions can change very quickly.

Cambridge Global English Stage 8 Workbook

17 Summer season

Summer holidays

1 Make nine compound nouns to do with holidays by finding words in word square A and matching them with words in word square B. (One word in word square A is used twice.)

A

I	N	T	T	O	C	C	S
N	F	A	Y	R	A	P	L
S	U	B	T	S	M	I	E
E	U	L	M	S	P	C	E
C	J	E	Y	U	I	N	P
T	R	D	Z	N	N	I	I
I	C	O	O	L	G	C	N
M	F	O	L	D	I	N	G

B

R	E	P	E	L	L	E	N	T
M	H	H	C	N	X	B	R	E
H	C	T	H	B	G	Y	J	N
A	R	A	A	A	V	Y	L	N
T	E	V	I	G	N	O	F	I
K	A	G	R	K	T	C	L	S
B	M	Q	X	K	K	E	R	F
O	Q	I	B	A	S	K	E	T
X	O	H	O	L	I	D	A	Y

2 Replace each of the underlined phrases in these sentences with an informal phrase from the box.

1 You can play table tennis and football, you can go swimming, and <u>do other similar activities</u>.
_____

2 <u>In addition</u>, you can go swimming at night.
_____

3 Barbecues <u>aren't enjoyable</u> when it rains.
_____

4 Camping holidays <u>aren't my favourite kind of holiday</u>.
_____

5 <u>I enjoy</u> surfing <u>very much</u>.
_____

6 I just want to <u>relax</u> on holiday.
_____

- aren't much fun
- aren't really for me
- that kind of thing
- the other thing is that
- chill out
- I'm really into

Cambridge Global English Stage 8 Workbook

17: Summer season

3 Complete what each person is saying or thinking with a phrase from the box below. You will need to solve the anagram in each phrase.

1. Three weeks is too long for a holiday. _____

2. We had a great time at the water park! _____

3. We had a room overlooking the sea. _____

4. My mum enjoyed the holiday. _____

5. _____ But they made lots of new friends on holiday.

6. I hate camping. _____

---

i n c e
- It was a very _____ view.

r e b o d
- I'm so _____.

n u f
- It was really _____.

c o l i b a s e
- My grandparents aren't normally very _____.

b o r n o t e c u f l a m
- It's just so _____ sleeping on the ground.

d e r a l e x
- She said she felt really _____.

Summer camp in Japan

1 Complete the text with the words from the box.

- accommodate
- dietary needs
- equipped with
- get-away
- natural setting
- overlooking
- purest
- ultimate
- fun

Cascade Alpine Resort

This is the perfect ¹ ___get-away___ for families who don't want to lie on the beach all day. Enjoy the ² _____ activity holiday with your family in the beautiful ³ _____ of the Alps and have some serious ⁴ _____. Stay in one of our luxurious wooden chalets ⁵ _____ comfortable beds and everything you need to make your stay enjoyable. There is an excellent restaurant, ⁶ _____ the waterfall, where our top chef will be pleased to ⁷ _____ all your ⁸ _____. Drink the ⁹ _____ ice-cold water from our own springs and breathe in the wonderful mountain air.

2 Match the two parts of each sentence by joining them with *should have / shouldn't have*, *would have / wouldn't have* or *could have / couldn't have* and the past participle of the verb in brackets.

1 I'm not surprised that you're tired. You ___shouldn't have stayed up so late___.

2 I've got stomach ache. I _____

3 I wish I had chosen the nature craft activity because I _____

4 If the weather hadn't been so horrible, we _____

5 If they'd chosen an activity holiday, they _____

- (climb) through the trees on high ropes and (go) on a night canoeing trip.
- (eat) so much at the barbecue.
- (enjoy) making things out of wood and leaves.
- (come) home early.
- (stay up) so late.

Cambridge Global English Stage 8 Workbook

17: Summer season

3 Solve the crossword.

Across

1 A friendly way to greet someone: '_____ to Cascade Alpine Resort!' (7)
7 An adjective which means 'from the evening until the following morning'. (9)
9 A large inland area of water. (4)
10 You can make it out of wood and it floats on water. (4)
11 Cycling, but not on roads. (8, 6)
12 Insects you can see at night. (9)

Down

2 '_____ games' are activities you do outside. (7)
3 The first meal of the day. (9)
4 It's smaller than a town. (7)
5 It's smaller than a mountain. (4)
6 Travelling on a lake or river in a narrow boat which can accommodate one person or more. (8)
8 Walking long distances. (6)

4 You wish you had gone on this holiday. Use *I could have* and *I would have* to say why. Write a paragraph in your notebook.

We went on a fantastic holiday to Australia. We went to Wilsons Promontory, which is in south-east Australia. We camped at a beautiful campsite with amazing views. We learned to surf and we went snorkelling. We went canoeing and we had picnics on the beach. We went on an overnight hike. We saw wildlife, such as koala bears, kangaroos and wombats. We had a great time!
 I wish I had gone with my friend to Wilsons Promontory. I could have camped at . . .

A room with a view

1 Make these direct questions more polite by writing them as indirect questions.

1 Has there been a phone message for me?
   Do you know if there has been a phone message for me?

2 What time is breakfast served?
   Could you tell me what time breakfast is served?

3 Is there a bus stop near the hotel?
   Could you tell me _____

4 How much would a taxi to the station cost?
   Do you know _____

5 Does the restaurant serve dinner on Sunday evenings?
   Could you tell me _____

6 Where is the nearest shopping centre?
   Do you know _____

2 Complete the sentences to say what these people are thinking.

1

I wonder _what the hotel will be like_.

2

I don't know _if dinner is included in the price_.

3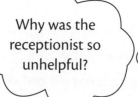

I wonder _____.

4

I don't know _____.

5

I'm not sure _____.

6

Will the weather be good in the morning?

I wonder _____.

17: Summer season

7 Should we go mountain biking tomorrow?

I wonder _____ .

8 What time does the restaurant close?

I'm not sure _____ .

9 Was this the campsite we stayed at last year?

I can't remember _____ .

3 Give the opposite of these adjectives by putting the correct prefix in front of them. Use a dictionary to help you.

1 _____ happy
2 _____ friendly
3 _____ tidy
4 _____ sociable
5 _____ patient
6 _____ possible
7 _____ polite
8 _____ honest
9 _____ loyal
10 _____ organised
11 _____ dependent
12 _____ formal

Adjectival prefixes

Prefixes are letters that come at the beginning of a word. Some prefixes are used with adjectives to give them a negative or opposite meaning. They include:

dis-   im-   in-   un-

Remember which prefix to use, and learn the adjectives in pairs:

comfortable   uncomfortable

You can say, for example, 'the bed wasn't comfortable'. But it shows you have a good command of English if you can use the correct prefix: 'the bed was uncomfortable'.

Study skills

4 Use the adjectives you wrote in Exercise 3 to complete these sentences.

1 The room was a real mess. The room was very ____*untidy*____ .
2 You can wear T-shirts and shorts in the restaurant. It's very _____ here.
3 I'm sorry, but we seem to have lost your booking details. I do apologise. We're not normally so _____ .
4 I'm sorry you don't like your room. We don't want our guests to be _____ , so we can offer you a different room at the same price.
5 We have apartments equipped with cooking facilities for guests who prefer to be _____ .

Cambridge Global English Stage 8 Workbook

18 Using English

King Midas

1 Complete the text with the words from the box.

| • auditioned | • acting | • director | • play |
| • script | • stage manager | • stage school | • play the part |

I'm really keen on ¹_____. I go to a ²_____ on Saturday mornings and after school on Wednesdays. Last week, I ³_____ for a part in a ⁴_____ at the local theatre. I was sent the ⁵_____ in advance, so I knew what it was about. I was interviewed by two people: the ⁶_____, who has directed a lot of plays at the theatre, and the ⁷_____. I was quite nervous, but it went well. They want me to ⁸_____ of a difficult teenager. My mum said that wouldn't be difficult!

2 Report the underlined questions, statements and commands.

Director: Hello, Emma. Thanks for coming. Now, you got the script? ¹Do you like the story?

Emma: Yes, I did. I thought it was really interesting. ²I like the character of Lara.

Director: OK. that's fine. ³Will you read the part of Lara, please?

Emma: Yes. ⁴Where do you want me to start?

Director: ⁵Start at the top of the page.

Emma: OK.

Director: ⁶Don't be nervous. Take your time. ⁷Speak up because your voice needs to reach the back of the room.

1 He asked her _if she liked the story_.
2 She said _____.
3 He asked her _____.
4 She asked him _____.
5 He told her _____.
6 He told her _____.
7 He told her _____.

106 Cambridge Global English Stage 8 Workbook

3 Look at the posters and answer the questions.

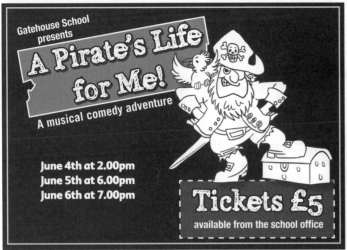
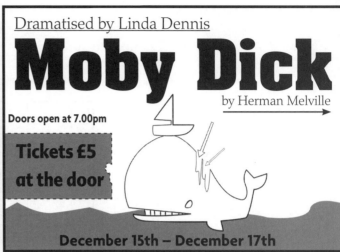

1 Which play has an afternoon performance?
   _____

2 Which play is about a whale?
   _____

3 Which play will make you laugh?
   _____

4 Which two plays would suit someone who enjoys singing?
   _____

5 Which play could you still get a part in?
   _____

6 Who was Herman Melville?
   _____

7 Who wrote the original version of *The Emperor's New Clothes*?
   _____

8 For which play do you **not** need to buy tickets in advance?
   _____

9 For which play can you buy tickets online?
   _____

10 What do Paul Russell and Linda Dennis have in common?
   _____

The story of Midas

1 Solve the crossword.

Across

2 Near or next to something. (12)
6 The official home of a king or queen and the people who live with them. (5)
7 The opposite of liquid. (5)
11 A model that looks like a person or animal, usually made from stone or metal. (6)
12 A _____ person makes good decisions based on knowledge and experience. (4)
15 Brought back together. (8)
17 The way in which you do something when you don't really want to do it. (11)
18 Very old. (7)
19 To walk without a particular direction or purpose. (6)

Down

1 A country with a king or queen. (7)
3 Something that is morally wrong or against the law. A criminal is guilty of this. (5)
4 Very important to you, very valuable. (8)
5 Something that is given. (4)
7 Origin, the place where a river starts. (6)
8 Kindness you show towards guests to make them feel welcome. (11)
9 The feeling of having no hope. (7)
10 Very pleased. (9)
13 Straightaway, now, without waiting. (11)
14 Part of a tree that grows out from the trunk. (6)
16 A large house where a king or queen lives. (6)
20 Very worried. (7)

2 Rewrite the passage putting in commas, full stops and capital letters where necessary.

we're doing a play at the end of term it's called the golden touch it's about a king with the power to turn everything to gold

this is what happens in the story after making everything in his palace turn to gold the king holds out his hand to his daughter realising too late that she will turn to gold the king is horrified and asks to lose his special power his daughter is brought back to life

i think it's a good story because it makes you realise that you should be very careful about what you wish for although you may be rich you may also be very unhappy

_____

3 Write the missing word in each sentence.

• a	• eyes	• in	• lesson	• made
• return	• soon	• sorry	• upon	• way

1 '*Once* _____ *a time*' is a phrase with which many traditional stories begin.
2 I'll call you *as* _____ *as* I get home.
3 Sit down and rest *for* _____ *while*.
4 He was late because he had *lost his* _____.
5 It was such a surprise. I *couldn't believe my* _____.
6 I think you've _____ *a mistake*.
7 I wouldn't want to do a parachute jump *for all the money* _____ *the world*.
8 He *felt* _____ *for* his mum because she had to work on her birthday.
9 He wouldn't ski off-piste again. He had *learned his* _____.
10 What can I do *in* _____ *for* your kindness?

Improving your writing style

You can make your writing more varied and interesting by including collocations, such as the ones in italics in Exercise 3.

Study skills

The performance

1 Here is an example script for the play *The Golden Touch*. Complete it in your own words.

THE GOLDEN TOUCH

SCENE 1 *The countryside near Midas's palace*

NARRATOR, TWO FARM WORKERS, SILENUS

NARRATOR: _____, there was a king called Midas. He ruled over the ancient kingdom of Phrygia. One day, two farm workers brought an old man to him. His name was Silenus. He had lost his way and was wandering in the countryside when they found him.

Silenus is wandering round, looking lost.

SILENUS: Where am I? I'm lost. Please help me! I'm an old man and I'm tired. I don't know where I am.

Enter two farm workers.

FARM WORKER 1: Look. There's an old man over there. He's lost.

FARM WORKER 2: Let's go and talk to him. Perhaps we can help him.

FARM WORKER 1: Are you lost? Can we help you?

SILENUS: _____. I don't know where I am.

FARM WORKER 2: What's your name?

SILENUS: My name is Silenus. I'm from Lydia.

FARM WORKER 1: _____. Perhaps someone there can help you.

Midas's palace

MIDAS: Silenus, welcome! You must stay here at my palace and rest for a while before you return to Lydia.

SILENUS: Thank you. You're very kind. I appreciate your generous hospitality.

MIDAS: Not at all. But tell me, _____ _____?

SILENUS: It's a long story, Your Majesty.

SCENE 2 *Lydia*

NARRATOR, MIDAS, SILENUS AND DIONYSUS

NARRATOR: When Silenus was fit and strong again, Midas took him back to his home in Lydia, a neighbouring kingdom. There, Silenus was reunited with one of his young students, Dionysus.

MIDAS: Here we are. _____ _____?

SILENUS: Here he is.

DIONYSUS: Silenus, here you are at last. We were all very anxious about you. We wondered where you were.

SILENUS: I lost my way and I was wandering in Phrygia for several days until I was taken to King Midas's palace. He kindly invited me to stay and I enjoyed his generous hospitality until I was fit and strong again.

DIONYSUS: In return for your kindness, King Midas, choose a gift – anything you want.

MIDAS: Let me see. _____ _____?

DIONYSUS: Are you sure that is what you want? Think about it very carefully.

MIDAS: Yes, I'm sure.

DIONYSUS: Well, if that really is what you want …

SCENE 3 *On the road between Lydia and Phrygia*

NARRATOR, MIDAS

NARRATOR: Midas decided to test his new gift immediately.

MIDAS: I wonder if I really have the power to turn everything I touch to gold? Let's see what happens when I touch the branch of this tree.

He touches the branch and it turns to gold.

NARRATOR: Midas couldn't believe his eyes.

MIDAS: _____!

He picks up a stone and it turns to gold.

MIDAS: It's incredible!

He picks an apple from a tree and it turns to gold.

MIDAS: It's gold. A golden apple!

He washes his hands in the water from a spring.

MIDAS: Even the water turns to liquid gold. I will be the richest man in the world.

SCENE 4 *Midas's palace*

MIDAS, TWO SERVANTS, AURELIA (MIDAS'S DAUGHTER)

MIDAS: I'm hungry and thirsty. Bring me something to eat. _____.

SERVANT 1: Yes, Your Majesty.

The servant brings some bread and offers it to Midas. Midas takes the bread.

MIDAS: I can't eat this. It's turned to gold. Bring me some meat.

SERVANT 2: Yes, Your Majesty.

The servant brings some meat and offers it to Midas. Midas takes the meat.

MIDAS: This has turned to gold too. _____.

SERVANT 1: Yes, Your Majesty.

The servant brings some water and offers it to Midas. Midas takes the water.

MIDAS: I can't drink it. Even the water has turned to gold.

Enter Aurelia.

AURELIA: Father, what's wrong?

Aurelia runs towards her father and puts her arms around him. She turns into a golden statue.

MIDAS: Oh, my daughter, my beautiful daughter! What have I done? If only I hadn't asked for the golden touch!

SCENE 5 *Midas's palace*

DIONYSUS, MIDAS, AURELIA (AS A STATUE)

DIONYSUS: Midas, how are you? _____ _____?

MIDAS: I made a terrible mistake. I shouldn't have asked for the golden touch. I wanted to be the richest man in the world but I'm now the poorest. I've lost what is most precious to me.

DIONYSUS: Which would you rather have, a cup of cold water or the golden touch?

MIDAS: A cup of water.

DIONYSUS: Which would you rather have, a piece of bread or the golden touch?

MIDAS: _____.

DIONYSUS: Do you want to have your daughter back, or do you want to have all the gold in the world?

MIDAS: My daughter, my daughter, my beautiful child!

SCENE 6 *Near the source of the River Pactolus*

NARRATOR, DIONYSUS, MIDAS

NARRATOR: Dionysus felt sorry for Midas and he knew that the king had learned a useful lesson.

DIONYSUS: Come, Midas. This is the River Pactolus. You must go to its source and put your hands in the water to wash away your crime.

MIDAS: _____.

He goes to the river and puts his hands in the water. The river turns to gold.

Enter Aurelia (as herself).

MIDAS: Aurelia!

AURELIA: Father!

MIDAS: Come with me. All the gold in the world isn't as precious as you are to me. We'll live a simple, happy life in the country.

NARRATOR: And they lived happily ever after!

THE END

Grammar reference

Grammar: Unit 1

all

- Use *all* to talk about three or more people or things. Use *all* with a plural verb.

All students are welcome at the meeting.

- Use *all* without *of* before nouns or adjective + noun.

All new students must go to the school office.

- Use *all of* before pronouns.

All of us speak English.

- You can use *all* or *all of* before *the, my/your*, etc. and *this/that*.

All (of) my friends like football.

both

- Use *both* to talk about two people or things.

Both my mother and my father are bilingual.

- Use *both* with a plural noun and a plural verb.

In Quebec, in Canada, people speak French and English. Both languages are official languages.

- Use *both* without *of* before nouns.

Italian and Spanish are similar. Both languages are Latin languages.

- Use *both of* before the pronouns *us, you, them*.

Both of us want to go to university.

- You can use *both* or *both of* before *the, my/your*, etc. and *these/those*.

Both (of) my sisters are studying Medicine.

each and *every*

- Use *each* for two or more people or things.

There are two English classrooms. Each classroom has an interactive whiteboard.

- Use *every* for three or more people or things.

Every student can learn two or more languages at this school.

- Use *each* and *every* with singular nouns and verbs.

Each/Every word is important in this poem.

- Use *every* when you're thinking of groups or large numbers.

They gave every student the same poem to read.

- Use *each* when you're thinking of things which are separate or different.

Each student found a different meaning in the poem.

- Use *each of* before the pronouns *us, you, them*.

Each of them did well in the end-of-term exam.

- Use *each of* before *the, my/your*, etc. and *these/those*.

I phone each of my grandmothers once a week.

Use *every one of* before *the, my/your*, etc, and *these/those*.

Every one of my friends has got a smartphone.

neither

Use *neither* to talk about two things.

Neither of my parents learned English at school.

Use *neither* with a singular or plural verb.

Neither of my parents has/have been to London.

Neither of them has/have been to London.

Grammar: Unit 2

will future, passive form

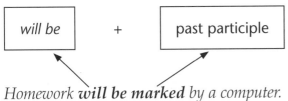

Homework **will be marked** by a computer.

should have + past participle

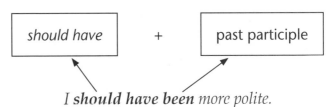

I **should have been** more polite.

Infinitive	Past simple	Past participle
be	was/were	been
become	became	become
begin	began	begun
bite	bit	bitten
blow	blew	blown
break	broke	broken
bring	brought	brought
build	built	built
buy	bought	bought
catch	caught	caught
choose	chose	chosen
come	came	come
cost	cost	cost
cut	cut	cut
do	did	done
draw	drew	drawn
drink	drank	drunk
drive	drove	driven
eat	ate	eaten
fall	fell	fallen
feed	fed	fed
feel	felt	felt
fight	fought	fought
find	found	found
fly	flew	flown
forget	forgot	forgotten
get	got	got
give	gave	given
go	went	gone/been
grow	grew	grown
have	had	had
hear	heard	heard
hit	hit	hit
hold	held	held
hurt	hurt	hurt
keep	kept	kept

Infinitive	Past simple	Past participle
know	knew	known
leave	left	left
lend	lent	lent
lose	lost	lost
make	made	made
meet	met	met
pay	paid	paid
put	put	put
read	read	read
ride	rode	ridden
ring	rang	rung
run	ran	run
say	said	said
see	saw	seen
sell	sold	sold
send	sent	sent
shine	shone	shone
shut	shut	shut
sing	sang	sung
sit	sat	sat
sleep	slept	slept
speak	spoke	spoken
spend	spent	spent
stand	stood	stood
steal	stole	stolen
swim	swam	swum
take	took	taken
teach	taught	taught
tell	told	told
think	thought	thought
throw	threw	thrown
understand	understood	understood
wake (up)	woke (up)	woken (up)
wear	wore	worn
win	won	won
write	wrote	written

Cambridge Global English Stage 8 Workbook

Grammar: Unit 3

Relative clauses

A clause is a part of a sentence.

The Amazon River Basin, <u>which lies just below the equator</u>, covers about 40% of South America.

This is a relative clause. We call it a **non-defining relative clause** because it gives extra information. The information is not essential, but it's interesting.

People managed to escape the massive wave <u>which/that was caused by an earthquake</u>.

This is also a relative clause. We call it a **defining relative clause** because it defines exactly what we're talking about. It is essential to the meaning. In this case, we're talking about the particular wave that was caused by an earthquake.

Relative pronouns: *who, which, that*

	Use *who* for people. The word *who* **replaces** *he, she* or *they*.	Use *which* or *that* for things. The word *which* or *that* **replaces** *it* or *they*.
	who	*which/that*
Non-defining relative clauses	Francisco de Orellana, who came from Extremadura in Spain, led an expedition down the Amazon River in 1542.	The Amazon River, which starts in Peru, flows through six countries in South America.
Defining relative clauses	I met the girl who rang the emergency bell.	It was her quick thinking which saved people's lives.

Leaving out relative pronouns

When a relative pronoun (*which, that, who*) is the **object** of the verb which follows, we can put it in or leave it out. However, we can't leave out a relative pronoun when it is the **subject** of the verb which follows.

The report that I read said no one had died.

The report I read said no one had died.   *The report that said no one had died was wrong.*

the object of the verb *read*   the subject of the verb *said*

Cambridge Global English Stage 8 Workbook

Grammar: Unit 4

Past simple

Use the past simple for something that happened at a particular time in the past and is completed. We often use the past simple with time expressions such as *yesterday, last weekend, on Monday, two years ago*. A lot of past simple verbs are irregular. On page 113, there is a list of irregular past tenses.

Present perfect

Use the present perfect for
- something that started in the past that has a present result:

I've bought you a present.
- something that started in the past and continues up to now:

I've been at this school for two years.
- recent events or actions:

I've finished my homework.

We often use the present perfect with expressions such as *ever, never, already* and *yet*.

Past continuous

Use the past continuous for something that was happening around a particular time in the past:

What were you doing at this time yesterday?

Use the past continuous with the past simple to talk about something that was happening when something else happened:

I was walking down the street when I saw my English teacher.

Compare these two sentences:

1 *I was having dinner when the storm started.*

2 *I had dinner when the storm started.*

In sentence 1 you had already started eating your dinner and then the storm started.

In sentence 2 you started to eat your dinner at the same time as (or soon after) the storm started.

Past simple passive

Use the past simple passive when you don't know who did the action, or when it's not important to know who did it:

The flight was cancelled because of poor weather conditions.

Past perfect simple

Use the past perfect simple for something that happened before another event in the past:

We had already set out for the airport when the storm started.

Grammar: Unit 5

Abstract nouns

An abstract noun is a noun which refers to a quality, an idea or a feeling.

> "**Friendship** ... is not something you learn in school. But if you haven't learned the meaning of friendship, you really haven't learned anything."
> Muhammed Ali, boxer

quality	idea	feeling
determination	beauty	happiness
kindness	education	disappointment
strength	freedom	fear

We usually use abstract nouns without *the* or *a/an*. However, when you make an abstract noun specific rather than general, you use *the* or *a/an*:

You need **determination** to be successful.

She's only 12 years old, but she has **the determination of someone twice her age.**

Present perfect continuous

Use the present perfect continuous to talk about actions continuing up to now, especially with *for* and *since* to say how long they have lasted.

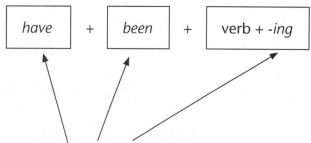

We've been living here for three years.
I've been playing the flute since I was eight.

You can also use the present perfect continuous for continuous actions in the past that have a present result:

Your hair's wet. Have you been swimming?
You aren't hungry because you've been eating sweets all day.

Grammar: Unit 6

Position of adverbs

Adverbs of frequency

always, often, usually/normally, sometimes, never

Adverbs of certainty

certainly, definitely, probably

Other useful adverbs

already, also, only, just, still, even

These adverbs go **before** main verbs:

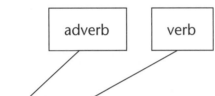

I **usually read** for a while before I go to sleep.

I **definitely want** to study music at college.

I **only took up** the piano last year.

However, the adverbs go **after** the verb *be* and auxiliary verbs and modals, e.g. *have, will, can, must, should,* etc.

I'**m usually** in bed by 9.30.

I'**ve never** been to the circus.

You **should definitely** try snowboarding. You'd really enjoy it.

Grammar: Unit 7

Phrasal verbs: word order

You can say:

Switch the TV off.

OR

Switch off the TV.

Turn the volume down.

OR

Turn down the volume.

But if the object is a pronoun (for example, *it* rather than *the TV*), you must separate the two parts of the verb:

Switch it off.

NOT

~~Switch off it.~~

Turn it down.

NOT

~~Turn down it.~~

Comparative adjectives with *much*, etc.

These are some rules for making comparative adjectives:

- for most one-syllable adjectives ending in *-e*, add *-r* — **close > closer**
- for other one-syllable adjectives, add *-er* — **long > longer**
- for two-syllable adjectives ending in *-y*, change the *y* to *i* and add *-er* — **easy > easier**
- for other two-syllable adjectives, use *more* in front of the adjective — **useful > more useful**
- for longer adjectives, use *more* in front of the adjective — **convenient > more convenient**

When an adjective ends in a single vowel and a single consonant, and the final syllable is stressed, double the consonant before adding *-er* — **big > bigger**

To make comparisons between things that are equal, use *as ... as*:

Your garden's **as big as** a football pitch!

To make negative comparisons use *less ... than* or *not as ... as*:

The blender is **less expensive than** the food processor.

The blender is**n't as expensive as** the food processor.

To make comparisons stronger, use:

much	You're much neater than I am. You're much more helpful at home than I am. (OR ... than me)
far ... than	The kitchen is far bigger than the dining room.
a lot less ... than	The new dishwasher's a lot less noisy than the old one.
nowhere near as ... as	My room's nowhere near as colourful as yours.
just as ... as	My room's just as messy as your room.

Cambridge Global English Stage 8 Workbook

Grammar: Unit 8

The present passive

In scientific and technical writing, the passive is often used.

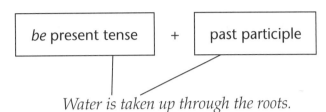

Water is taken up through the roots.

We use the passive because we want to focus on the action, not the person or thing that does the action.

positive	negative	questions	short answers
Oxygen is released.	Carbon dioxide isn't released.	Is oxygen released?	Yes, it is. / No, it isn't.

For a list of irregular past participles, see page 113.

The present perfect passive

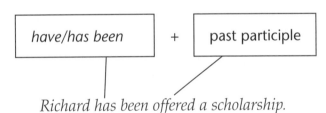

Richard has been offered a scholarship.

We also use the passive when we don't know who does the action, or when it isn't important to know.

positive	negative	questions	short answers
The lion lights have been used in Kenya.	The lions haven't been killed.	Have the lion lights been used?	Yes, they have. / No, they haven't.

If we want to say who does the action, we can use *by*:

Richard has been offered a scholarship by the headteacher at one of Kenya's top schools.

Grammar: Unit 9

Questions beginning with prepositions

Prepositions are words like *to, at, from, by, on, about*. In conversation, prepositions usually come at the end of a question: *Which cinema did you go to? Where did you get your shoes from? What were you talking about?*

In formal language and in sentences which are complex, it is sometimes clearer to put the preposition at the beginning of the question: *On which building is there a roof designed to look like the sails on a ship?*

Past continuous

Use the past continuous to say that something was happening around a particular time in the past.

Past continuous active

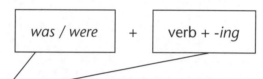

We were driving across the bridge when a rainbow appeared.

	positive	negative	questions	short answers
Past continuous active	We were driving.	We weren't walking.	Were you driving?	Yes, we were. / No, we weren't.

Past continuous passive

We use the passive when we don't know who does the action, or when it isn't important to know.

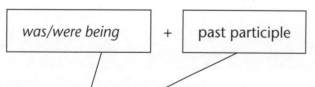

The bridge was being built when we went to France.

	positive	negative	questions	short answers
Past continuous passive	The bridge was being built when we went to France.	It wasn't being used because it wasn't finished.	Was the bridge being built?	Yes, it was, / No, it wasn't.

For a list of irregular past participles, see page 113.

Grammar: Unit 10

Quantifiers with countable and uncountable nouns

Containers

a **packet** of biscuits, rice, sweets

a **box** of chocolates, matches, cereal, tissues, biscuits

a **jar** of jam, peanut butter, olives

a **carton** of yogurt, milk, fruit juice, ice cream

a **bottle** of water, lemonade, olive oil

a **can** of cola

a **tin** of tomatoes, soup, biscuits

a **bag** of crisps

Pieces

a **bar** of chocolate, soap

a **loaf** of bread

a **slice** of cake, cold meat, cheese, toast

a **lump** of sugar

Sets

a **bunch** of bananas, flowers, grapes

a **pack** of cards

a **crowd** of people

a **flock** of sheep

a **herd** of cattle

Plural nouns

Spelling change: *f* to *v*

loaf	loaves	wife	wives
shelf	shelves	half	halves
knife	knives	wolf	wolves
life	lives		

Singular and plural the same

sheep

fish

salmon

deer

Irregular plurals

child	children
man	men
woman	women
foot	feet
tooth	teeth
mouse	mice

Singular nouns ending in *s* (followed by a verb in the singular)

athletics   *Athletics **is** ...*

economics

gymnastics

physics

politics

mathematics

news

Plural nouns with no singular (followed by a verb in the plural)

people   *People **are** ...*

clothes

trousers

thanks

police

congratulations

cattle

Grammar: Unit 11

Adjectives followed by prepositions

Adjectives sometimes have prepositions after them. It's helpful to learn them as whole phrases.

I'm **afraid of** spiders.

They were **angry about** the referee's decision.

Don't be **angry with** me. I was doing my best.

Don't get **anxious about** the exam. You'll be fine.

I'm **bad at** tennis. I haven't got good hand–eye co-ordination.

A Canadian accent is **different from** an American accent.

I'm a bit **disappointed with** my exam results. I should have done better.

We're very **excited about** the trip to Paris.

Are you **frightened of** spiders?

She's very **good at** Maths.

I'm **interested in** archaeology.

Thank you. That's very **kind of** you.

Your uncle and aunt were very **kind to** me when I stayed with them.

I'm **pleased about** the new timetable. It means we don't have to get to school so early.

I'm **pleased with** my new phone. It's better than my old one.

It's good to know enough of a foreign language so that you can be **polite to** people.

He got into trouble because he was **rude to** a teacher.

I'm **sorry about** the mess. I'll clear it up.

I feel really **sorry for** my friend. She's broken her leg so she can't go on holiday.

We were **surprised at/by** how expensive everything was in London.

This cheese is very **typical of** the region.

What's **wrong with** you today? You're a bit quiet.

Prepositions followed by nouns

Nouns sometimes have prepositions before them. It's helpful to learn them as whole phrases. Notice that some nouns need *the*.

at (the age of) 15

at school/university/college

at home

at night/midnight

at the cinema/the theatre

at the weekend

by car/bus/bike, etc.

by Shakespeare/Tolstoy

in the morning/the afternoon/the evening

in pen/pencil

in the news

in time (*We arrived in time to catch the train*)

on time (*The train arrived on time*)

on the radio

on TV

Grammar: Unit 12

Verbs followed by verb + -ing

(don't) mind	finish
admit	give up
avoid	imagine
can't help	involve
can't stand	keep (on)
consider	miss
delay	practise
deny	risk
enjoy	spend time
fancy	suggest
feel like	

I **enjoy going** to the cinema.

Do you **fancy going** to the cinema tonight?

Prepositions followed by verb + -ing

Use the *-ing* form after all prepositions.

You're very good **at making** things.

Thank you **for helping** me.

I'm keen **on riding**.

Do you feel **like playing** tennis?

will future

Use *will* for giving information about the future and for predicting what we think or guess will happen.

positive	I'm looking forward to the trip. It'll be really interesting.
negative	You won't be bored.
questions	Will it be hot and sunny?
short answers	Yes, it will. / No, it won't.

Future continuous

Use the future continuous for saying that something will be in progress at a time in the future:

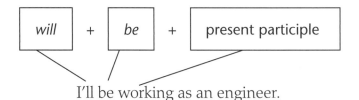

I'll be working as an engineer.

positive	By the time I'm 30, I'll be working as an engineer.
negative	I won't be studying for exams.
questions	Will you be living in this country?
short answers	Yes, I will. / No, I won't.

Grammar: Unit 13

Reflexive pronouns

subject pronoun	reflexive pronoun
I	myself
you	yourself
he/she/it	himself, herself, itself
we	ourselves
you	yourselves
they	themselves

Use reflexive pronouns with verbs when the object is the same person (or thing) as the subject:

I fell over, but I didn't hurt myself.

Parrots like looking at themselves in the mirror.

Do not use reflexive pronouns with these verbs:

get up, wash, feel, relax, hurry

Notice the difference between:

They looked at themselves. (They looked at their own reflection in a mirror.)

AND

They looked at each other. (Each person looked at the other person.)

Notice also:

They have known each other for a long time.

NOT

They have known themselves for a long time.

You can use reflexive pronouns to emphasise the subject or object:

I made this cake myself.

Did you paint your room yourself?

Grammar: Unit 14

to have something done

If you have something done, someone does it for you. You don't do it yourself.

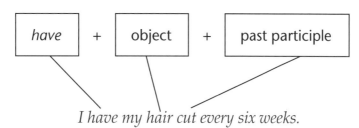

I have my hair cut every six weeks.

You can also use *get something done*. It means the same as *have something done*.

I get my hair cut every six weeks.

Past perfect in reported speech

When we tell people what someone said, we usually change the tense because what they said was in the past. If someone uses the present perfect in direct speech, we change it to the past perfect in reported speech.

"I've just read a book about Arctic explorers." → He said he'd just read a book about Arctic explorers.

"I haven't read a book about explorers before." → He said he hadn't read a book about explorers before.

If someone uses the past simple in direct speech, we also change it to the past perfect in reported speech.

"I wrote a book review for the school magazine." → He said he'd written a book review for the school magazine.

"I didn't write a short story." → He said he hadn't written a short story.

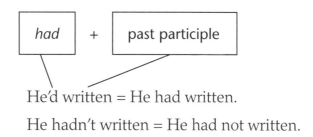

He'd written = He had written.

He hadn't written = He had not written.

Grammar: Unit 15

despite, in spite of

Despite and *in spite of* introduce contrasting ideas. Notice that you can put them at the beginning or in the middle of a sentence.

Despite / In spite of *their problems, they have continued to have a positive attitude.*

They have continued to have a positive attitude **despite / in spite of** *their problems.*

You can use *despite / in spite of* followed by an *-ing* form.

Despite / In spite of having *very little food and water, they are managing to survive.*

Modals

must and have to

Must and *have to* are similar in meaning.

Use *must* to express personal feelings:

I really loved that book. I must read it again. (I feel I really want to read the book again.)

Use *have to* to express obligations:

I have to read this book by Friday. (The teacher has told us to read this book by Friday.)

Use *must* or *have to* to talk about rules:

You must be at school by 8.30.

You have to be at school by 8.30.

Use *must* to talk about the present or the future, but not the past. If you want to talk about the past, use *had to*:

I had to finish the book. It was so exciting that I couldn't put it down.

mustn't and don't have to

Use *mustn't* to say what is not allowed:

You mustn't talk when the teacher's talking.

Use *don't have to* to say that something isn't necessary:

You don't have to be good at sport to enjoy it.

must and should

Use *must* to say that it is necessary to do something:

You must do your homework before you watch TV.

must has a stronger meaning than *should*:

You should do your homework before you watch TV. (It's a good idea to …)

Grammar: Unit 16

Comparative adverbs

To make comparative adverbs, use *more* + adverb (*than*).

*The rescue operation was reported **more widely than** previous mining rescue attempts.*

To make comparisons stronger, use *much*:

*It was reported **much more widely than** previous rescue attempts.*

The following comparatives are irregular:

adverb	comparative
well	better
badly	worse
far	further
much	more

Some comparatives of adverbs end in *-er*:

adverb	comparative
fast	faster
long	longer
high	higher
early	earlier
late	later
hard	harder
near	nearer
soon	sooner

Remember to use the base form of the adverb with (*not*) *as ... as*:

*I don't run **as fast as** you.* NOT *I don't run as faster as you.*

Grammar: Unit 17

Indirect and embedded questions

To ask for information and to make questions more polite, start with 'Do you know ... ?' or 'Could you tell me ... ?'

Remember to change the word order.

Where is the station?

Could you tell me where the station is?

Remember, too, that you don't use the auxiliaries *do*, *does* or *did*; and you must make the verb agree with the subject.

What time **does the bus leave**?

*Do you know what time **the bus leaves**?*

NOT

Do you know what time does the bus leave?

With *Yes/No* questions, use *if* or *whether*.

Is there a swimming pool at the hotel?

I wonder if/whether there's a swimming pool at the hotel.

Grammar: Unit 18

Reported speech: summary

When we tell people what someone said, we usually change the tense of the verb because what they said was in the past.

Statements	
am/are/is → was/were have/has → had can → could will → would do/does → did present simple → past simple past simple → past perfect present perfect → past perfect	Midas: "I'm delighted." → He said he was delighted. Midas: "I will be the richest man in the world." → He said he would be the richest man in the world.
Questions	
Change the tense and change the word order when you report questions.	Dionysus: "What do you want?" Dionysus asked him what he wanted. Dionysus: "Do you want all the gold in the world?" Dionysus asked him if he wanted all the gold in the world.
Commands	
Use *tell* or *ask* + object + *to* infinitive	Dionysus: "Choose a gift." Dionysus told him to choose a gift.

Capital letters

Use capital letters for the start of a sentence and for the first letter in:

- days
- months
- festivals
- countries
- people's titles
- nationalities and languages
- titles of books, plays and films